BERNARD
LONERGAN

AN

INTRODUCTORY

GUIDE TO *INSIGHT*

BERNARD LONERGAN

AN

INTRODUCTORY

GUIDE TO *INSIGHT*

Terry J. Tekippe

PAULIST PRESS
New York/Mahwah, N.J.

Cover design by Valerie Petro
Book design by Sharyn Banks and Theresa M. Sparacio

Library of Congress Cataloging-in-Publication Data

Tekippe, Terry J.
    Bernard Lonergan: an introductory guide to *Insight* / Terry J. Tekippe.
      p. cm
Includes index.
    ISBN 0-8091-4150-7
    1. Lonergan, Bernard J. F. *Insight*   2. Knowledge, Theory of.   I. Title.
B995.L653 I578 2003
121—dc21   2003004710

Published by Paulist Press
997 Macarthur Boulevard
Mahwah, New Jersey 07430

www.paulistpress.com

Printed and bound in the United States of America

Contents

Contents

Preface

Near the beginning of *Insight* Lonergan remarks that proposing a philosophy is like building a ship—there is no possibility of doing it halfway. That serves as a marvelous symbol of Lonergan's vaulting intellectual ambitions: he was never content to do something halfway.

Lonergan saw himself as an inheritor of the Aristotelian and Thomistic tradition. He followed these eminent thinkers, not only in their doctrines, but also in their omnivorous curiosity.

The Ambitions of Aristotle and Thomas

Aristotle systematized the philosophical work of Socrates and Plato. In a rigorously scientific expression, he explored the primary realities in his *Metaphysics*. He exhaustively analyzed the possibilities of logic and science in the *Prior* and *Posterior Analytics*. He investigated human knowing in *On the Soul,* and presented moral philosophy in the *Nicomachean Ethics.* He studied the history of his philosophical predecessors.

But his interests ranged wider. He summed up the science of his time in the *Physics* and ventured into biology in *On the Generation of Animals* and *On the Soul.* He explored statecraft, and made a collection of some 150 constitutions of various city-states. In short, his work constituted at least a sketch of what a total set of sciences would look like. Appropriately, Virgil introduces him to Dante in the *Inferno* as *il maestro di coloro che sanno*—the master of those who know.

Thomas Aquinas's knowledge was no less wide-ranging. He knew the scriptures intimately and had mastered the work of the church fathers, especially Augustine, but had pioneered as well in the study of the eastern fathers. He quickly absorbed the newly available works of Aristotle, grasping intuitively the thought of the one he called "the Philosopher," often through literal translations from the Greek or Arabic. On most of these works he wrote a commentary. He knew the great thinkers of the immediate past: Anselm of Canterbury, Bernard of Clairvaux, Abelard, Hugh of St. Victor and especially Peter Lombard, on whose *Sentences,* like all the medievals, he wrote his doctoral dissertation. He was familiar with the thought of his contemporaries, Philip the Chancellor, Albert the Great and Bonaventure. He had studied the great Muslim commentators of Aristotle, Avicenna, Alfarabi and Averroes, as well as his Jewish counterparts, Moses Maimonides and Isaac Israeli. He had a grasp of the canon law collections and commentaries, conciliar and papal teachings, but he was also au courant with the science of his day.

Lonergan's Ambition

At the end of *Insight* Lonergan recalls the years he had spent looking up to the mind of Aquinas. Between the lines, one reads Lonergan's own ambition: to do for the twentieth century what Thomas had done for the thirteenth and what Aristotle had attempted before him: to grasp all of human knowing and press it into a masterful synthesis.

The briefest survey of the explosion of human knowledge between the thirteenth and twentieth centuries, however, indicates the staggering challenge, if not the folly, of Lonergan's ambition. Besides the years of studying Thomas, Lonergan had to know the later medievals, especially Scotus and Ockham, and the Thomistic commentators Cajetan, John of St. Thomas, Capreolus, Bañez, Molina and Suarez, as well as the later Rousselot and Marechal.

Philosophy in the modern age entered a whole new phase of approach through the subject, requiring Lonergan to master Descartes, Leibniz, Hume, Kant, Locke, Fichte, Schelling, Hegel, Heidegger and Husserl.

More striking still was the rise of modern science in the seventeenth century, which transformed human knowing and human living and made obsolete all of Thomas Aquinas's scientific references. The twentieth century also saw the arrival of a statistical science to parallel a more classical approach, as well as relativity and quantum mechanics.

In the nineteenth century a revolution of historical consciousness took place, demanding a new standard of historical accuracy, a requirement that everything be grasped in terms of its development, and a wealth of historical data. In a similar way, Darwin proposed the historicity of species and initiated evolutionary thought.

In the same period, novel geometries were proposed as a rival to Euclid's; in the twentieth century, symbolic logic and mathematics tended to merge, as in Russell's and Whitehead's *Principia Mathematica*.

The earlier work of Adam Smith flowered in twentieth century economics, while sociology came into its own. The year 1900 saw the publication of Freud's *Traumdeutung, The Interpretation of Dreams,* which started a new study of empirical and depth psychology. Hermeneutics, the science of interpretation, came to the fore, as well as a sympathetic study of myth.

How could anyone dare attempt to cope with such a variety of fields of knowing, when many scientists admitted that they couldn't keep up with even their own field? Lonergan was not fazed by the challenge. Within the covers of *Insight,* astoundingly, he deals with all those fields, and more, managing to meld them all into a synthesis from the point of view of human knowing itself.

The original project was even vaster: Lonergan saw the philosophical work as but a precursor to a treatise on theological method; it was the call to teach in Rome that forced him to "round off" what he had already accomplished, and put off the theological method for another day. Perhaps it was just as well; otherwise, Lonergan might have had a 2,000 page tome for which he would never have found a publisher. As it was, he searched for four years before finding anyone willing to take a chance on *Insight.*

As it turned out, it was another twenty years between the completion of *Insight* and the publication of *Method in Theology* in 1972. Lung cancer, an operation to remove one lung, and a lengthy recuperation period intervened. In his later work, Lonergan offered much that was valuable and even brilliant, but, in my critical opinion, he never reached the heights of his earlier work. *Insight* remains his masterpiece.

Why Read Lonergan?

The sheer ambition and scope of Lonergan's project, of course, is what makes *Insight* such a difficult work. Lonergan rarely made a concession to his readers. One might well wonder why a person would tackle this work at all. No guarantee can be given in advance that the effort will be worthwhile. The reasons for reading *Insight* can only be stated, not proven. They can only be proven by the reader who goes through the labor of personally appropriating his challenging text. In the long run, they can only be proven by the test of history. But here they are:

1. Lonergan's *Insight* is one of the great philosophical works of the twentieth century. It easily compares to such works as Sartre's *Being and Nothingness,* Whitehead's *Process and Reality* or Heidegger's *Being and Time.* It does not appear to this writer to be premature to compare it to the masterpieces of philosophy: Hegel's *Phenomenology of Mind,* Kant's *Critique of Pure Reason,* Aristotle's *Metaphysics.* For this reason alone it will be of interest to the serious thinker.

2. Moreover, Lonergan proposes a philosophy that would seem attuned to the age. He takes the approach through the subject, which is characteristic of all modern philosophy since Descartes. He claims, in an empirical age, a philosophy that is empirically verifiable, and in an age dominated by the success of scientific method, a philosophy which is methodical, and not arrived at simply by grand intuitions.

3. In spite of its empirical starting point, Lonergan's philosophy is open to God and belief in God. Accepting and defending the claims of both reason and faith, Lonergan's philosophy should be of interest to any thinking Christian.

4. Lonergan's is a significant attempt of the Thomistic tradition to come to terms with modern philosophy and modern

science. Whether ultimately judging that effort to be a fulfillment or a betrayal of the tradition, any Thomist will find it a
project to be reckoned with.

5. More important than all of these is a personal issue. From
the deepest recesses of Greek culture comes the admonition,
"know thyself." The subtitle of Lonergan's work is *A Study of
Human Understanding*. But Lonergan is not talking about any
abstract understanding; he is not even talking just about his own
understanding; he is talking about the human understanding of
each and every one of his readers.

Some people buy a new car or a new computer and are perfectly happy just to operate it, as long as it does what it is supposed to do. But others are more curious about what goes on
"under the hood." Even more intimate to a person than a car or
a computer is his or her own knowing. Some may be perfectly
happy with what they already know of their knowing: Lonergan's work is not for them. But for those who would like to
know better the operations of their own minds, Lonergan's book
provides a profound and richly detailed answer. It is also an
answer, Lonergan insists, that is deeply significant for one's own
life. For to know one's knowing is already to know something
about, not just what has already been known, but what one will
ever know. The reader who finds that uninteresting should probably ignore Lonergan's work, while the reader who recognizes in
it a call may find that venturing into the challenges of Lonergan's
volume is worthwhile.

Introduction:
Some Practical Pointers

In the early 1970s, John Macquarrie, the well-known theologian, taught me at Union Theological. One day in class we got on to the subject of Lonergan's *Insight: A Study of Human Understanding.* "*Insight,*" Macquarrie exclaimed in his broad Scottish accent, "it's a j*ungle* of a book!"

Many a reader has had the same experience of this brilliant but challenging work, and the great danger is to miss the forest for the trees. The aim of this first reading guide is to avoid that difficulty, and to give the beginning reader a set of signposts to what is truly essential and central to the book.

The plan of the reading guide, accordingly, is not to cover everything, but to assign readings of only certain chapters, or even parts of chapters. This will allow one to focus on the main path through the maze, without getting distracted by a thousand byways. A general directive may be given that is valid for the whole book: What is not treated may, for a first reading, be safely ignored.

A special word must be said on the chapters on science in the early part of the work. These are the rocks on which many a reader without a specialized scientific background has been shipwrecked, and they are largely bypassed in this commentary. Nevertheless, the witness of contemporary science is too central to Lonergan's argument to be bypassed altogether, and so an attempt will be made to offer a minimally necessary coverage of that subject in the following text.

The reading guide is designed to be read first, followed by Lonergan's text. Ideally, the reader might want to read Lonergan's text first, study the commentary, and then return to a second reading of Lonergan's text.

A person totally unfamiliar with Lonergan's thought may find helpful the author's *What Is Lonergan Up to in Insight?* But the two books are written independently and do not have to be read together.

Lonergan's work is gradually being published in the *Collected Works* by the University of Toronto Press. *Insight* was published in volume 3 in 1992, and that is now the most critical text. Nevertheless, many still have or are familiar with the older edition, originally published by Longmans, Green and Co. in 1957. For that reason all pagination will be given first for the *Collected Works* edition, with the earlier pagination in parentheses.

At times it may be unclear whether a backward or forward reference is to Lonergan's work or this commentary. The following convention will be adopted: Lonergan's chapters will be referred to in Roman numerals, and the chapters of this commentary in Arabic numerals.

The Table of Contents of *Insight* will be reproduced here to offer some idea of what Lonergan will be treating.

Part I: Insight as Activity

I. Elements
  1. A Dramatic Instance
  2. Definition
  3. Higher Viewpoints
  4. Inverse Insight
  5. The Empirical Residue

II. Heuristic Structures of Empirical Method
  1. Mathematical and Scientific Insights Compared
  2. Classical Heuristic Structures
  3. Concrete Inferences from Classical Laws
  4. Statistical Heuristic Structures
  5. Survey

III. The Canons of Empirical Method
  1. The Canon of Selection

Chapter 1

Getting One's Bearings

READING: *Insight:* Preface; Introduction,
pp. 3–9, 11–24 (ix–xv, xvii–xxx)

A preface is usually written after the book: Once the whole has been completed, the writer returns to give a brief synopsis of his thought, sometimes expressed in a personal way. In this particular case, there is documentary evidence that the present preface is a second effort, written well after the book was completed.[1] But how can any book—much less one as complex as *Insight*—be communicated in a few pages? Lonergan formulates the problem well: "Indeed, this very wealth of implications is disconcerting, and I find it difficult to state in any brief and easy manner what the present book is about, how a single author can expect to treat the variety of topics listed on the table of contents, why he should attempt to do so in a single work, and what good he could hope to accomplish even were he to succeed in his odd undertaking."[2]

The following remarks on the preface and introduction, then, make no pretense to covering everything in these texts, but will merely highlight some of the most important themes for understanding *Insight*.

---

[1] For some remarks on the history of the two prefaces, see Frederick Crowe in *Method: Journal of Lonergan Studies*, March 1985. The same issue has the original preface, pp. 3–7.

[2] 3 (ix).

Preface: The Unity of Insight

Lonergan begins the preface with the example of the detective story. What he is singling out is the moment of insight. It is not any individual clue or even the memory of all the clues together. Insight is the "aha!" moment in which all the clues fall into place. "The thing takes shape," as Holmes was wont to say to Watson.

> In the ideal detective story, the reader is given all the clues yet fails to spot the criminal. He may advert to each clue as it arises and needs no further clues to solve the mystery. Yet he can remain in the dark for the simple reason that reaching the solution is not the mere apprehension of any clue, not the mere memory of all, but a quite distinct activity of organizing intelligence that places the full set of clues in a unique explanatory perspective.
>
> By insight, then, is meant not any act of attention or advertence or memory but the supervening act of understanding. 3(ix)

Insight, as will be seen, is not the whole of cognitional process, but for Lonergan it is the center and the key, providing even the title of the whole work. Much of the first part of the work will be devoted to grasping what an insight is.

The term *cognitional process* has been thrown around— what does it mean? It sounds very imposing and in fact its implications are impressive. Yet, in itself, it is something so ordinary and prosaic it hardly seems to deserve attention.

Cognitional process is simply the mind at work. It is what we refer to in everyday conversation when we say, "A penny for your thoughts!" "What's going on in that head of yours?" "Do you see what I mean?" "Are we thinking along the same lines?" "Do you see what I'm driving at?" "What is your final judgment on this question?"

Every person who is conscious has a private and privileged access to his own cognitional process. To be conscious is precisely to be aware of oneself, but also to be aware of one's own mental activities. It is these activities Lonergan is chiefly interested in. Among them insight is the center and the point of entry.

I remember when I was first challenged, as a philosophy student, to read *Insight*. "Have you ever seen the book?" I was asked. "Yes," I said, "I've looked through the table of contents, and I couldn't make heads or tails out of it." But my mistake was in focusing on the disparate contexts involved: the rods and clocks of physics, the emergent probability of history, the inhibition of depth psychology, the theories of the notion of being in metaphysics. But what ties this all together, Lonergan is suggesting in the preface, is the single act of insight. Physicists have their insights; so do historians and psychologists and metaphysicians. While I was focusing on the breathtaking diversity of these fields of knowing, Lonergan is pointing to the ever recurring act of insight that is taking place in each one of them.

Insight into Insight

Lonergan goes further, however, and says that the "aim of the work is to convey an insight into insight."[3] If "insight" at this point remains something of a murky notion, then "insight into insight" is probably murkiness squared. But a simple comparison may help. A video camera scans everything that passes before it. But the video camera can never focus on itself; by its physical construction the camera itself can never enter into its field of vision. But the mind is *not* like that. The mind does have a certain ability to be aware of its own action, to understand itself and to know itself. For Thomas Aquinas, this was a mark of the spiritual: It had an ability to return upon itself, and the more perfect the spiritual being, the more complete that return upon itself.

In most of our living, we are probably like the video camera, reflecting on what is passing before us in the carnival of life. But, unlike the video camera, we are also dimly aware of the workings

---

[3] 4 (ix).

of our mind, and it is that dim awareness Lonergan would call attention to and heighten.

If we do so, we can gradually come to understand more and more the conditions and qualifications, the antecedents and the consequences of the act of insight. To put it briefly, we can have an "insight into insight."

Once one has an insight into insight, then there is already a certain vague understanding in advance of all that there is to be understood. If, as Lonergan holds, all understanding takes place by the act of insight, then everything that will ever be understood will be understood by that same process of insight. Having grasped insight, one already knows something of that future process of understanding.

Implications of Insight into Insight

On this basis Lonergan, on pages 4–6 (x–xii), works out ten implications of insight into insight, notable among them that insight into insight will provide a philosophy and a metaphysics. How exactly that will take place, however, will probably have to remain a vague presentiment until the contents of the book are gradually unfolded.

Lonergan next lists three levels on which the book operates: "It is a study of human understanding. It unfolds the philosophic implications of understanding. It is a campaign against the flight from understanding." The first two correspond to the major division of the book: Part I, Insight as Activity, and Part II, Insight as Knowledge. As Lonergan later formulated it, "What do I do when I know?" That is the question about cognitional process, about the mental activities that take place in our minds when we know. Then, "What do I know when I do that?" Here the focus shifts from the activity to the content of knowing.

The third level, the campaign against the flight from understanding, may be more difficult to grasp. Besides understanding, there are times when we fail to understand—an experience quite as common as insight. But what is more perverse is that sometimes a person deliberately wants *not* to understand. There are some things we prefer not to know. If we have no responsibility to know them, that may be trivial. But in other cases this can be a "sin against the light." As we understand better the process of insight, so we also understand better how we avoid unwanted insights. In the commentary, however, the first two questions will receive the

> The question remains: What practical good can come of this book? The answer is more forthright than might be expected, for insight is the source not only of theoretical knowledge but also of all its practical applications, and indeed of all intelligent activity. Insight into insight, then, will reveal which activity is intelligent, and insight into oversights will reveal what activity is unintelligent. But to be practical is to do the intelligent thing, and to be unpractical is to keep blundering about. It follows that insight into both insight and oversight is the very key to practicality. 7–8 (xiii–xiv)

main emphasis; the third level of the flight from understanding will be given only a muted stress.

Introduction: Disjunction One

As Lonergan promises at the end of the preface, the introduction gives "a more exact account of the aim and structure of this book." He does this in five "disjunctions." The first will be taken by itself, the second and third together, and similarly the fourth and fifth.

As to the first, "the question is not whether knowledge exists but what precisely is its nature." This is not a total disjunction. The man on the street doesn't ask questions such as, "How do I know that I know?" But philosophers do ask such questions, and Lonergan cannot totally avoid them. Nevertheless, it is fair to say that, especially in the first part of the book, Lonergan's main preoccupation is with the how of knowing. As a geologist might theoretically start his investigations by asking, "Do rocks exist?" but is much more likely in reality simply to accept their existence, and start studying what kinds there are, so Lonergan largely assumes that knowing exists, and seeks to discover its kinds and its activities.

When Lonergan examines knowing, he discovers that there are really two basic kinds involved. Man is *animal rationalis* by the classic definition. He is an animal, and has a sense knowing in common with the other animals; he is also rational, possessing a power of reasoning and a spiritual intelligence that the other animals simply don't have.

Of course, Lonergan was not the first to discover this; it is a distinction that goes back at least to Plato. But I put it this way because it is crucial to understanding Lonergan's philosophy. For Lonergan, as can be seen in his treatment of the first disjunction, this dual knowing is the key to unraveling the whole history of philosophy. In Lonergan's thought, the question is not whether knowing exists; the problem rather is that there are two kinds of knowing, which are often confused. For the person of practical interests, focused on the world around him, the two kinds of knowing blur together in his awareness. But even philosophers are not immune to this confusion. Again according to Lonergan, empiricism is the perennial temptation of philosophy: to imagine that the rational and spiritual knowing is just like physical looking, or that there is a spiritual "look" by which we know reality. Lonergan expresses this tendency succinctly as "knowing is looking," and a polemic against this simplistic analysis runs through his work.

Disjunctions Two and Three

In the second and third disjunctions, Lonergan returns to a thought already found in the preface: This is not a book about mathematics, science, history or metaphysics. It is a book about insight. Of course, mathematicians, scientists, historians and metaphysicians have insights and to that extent their work is of interest. But the specific interest is not in those areas in themselves, but in the act of insight. That may be consolation to a reader who finds himself in over his head: The areas treated are only for the purposes of example.

This disjunction too, it may be noted, is not absolute. Despite his modest disclaimers, Lonergan was obviously a polymath and a genius. He had studied and thought through many areas, and he is clearly sharing the results of these varied investigations in *Insight,* hopeful of making a contribution to not a few fields. But, especially on a first reading, Lonergan should be taken rigorously at his word: The examples given are only that; if the reader finds them unhelpful, he should search for others. Even the failure to understand, if close attention is paid, can be instructive.

If the focus is not on the many fields of study, but on the act of insight, this means that what is important for Lonergan is something very personal. As stated earlier, every person has a private and privileged access to his or her own mental activities. For Lonergan, the crucial evidence for philosophy is what is going on in his or her head.

Sometimes philosophy is thought of as an abstract body of knowledge, gathered in dusty books, perhaps having little to do with the practical problems of living. This has probably never been true of philosophy at its best. Socrates, for example, lived and died for "reason." His greatest joy and delight was in a good intellectual discussion. When he was thrown in jail for "corrupting the youth," his friends came to him and urged him to flee; they were ready to bribe the proper guards and spirit him away. "Fine," he said to them, "just prove to me that it's the reasonable thing to do, and I will do it."

Lonergan's philosophy has some of that same personal challenge. It is not some foreign body or even someone else's mind that one is being invited to study, but one's own mind. "The evidence for philosophy is within you," to paraphrase the gospel. Lonergan calls it "self-appropriation": It is putting one's own house in order, discriminating carefully between the two kinds of knowing, being open and faithful to the intrinsic desire to know that is within each of us.

At this point Lonergan takes up an objection that mathematical and scientific examples may not be helpful to a particular reader.

He goes into a long disquisition on the reasons for appealing to science. But what is perhaps more important for the beginning reader is what he considers to be absolutely essential in the first part of the book. "In the first place, it is essential that the notion of insight, of the accumulation of insights, of higher viewpoints, and of their heuristic significance and implications, not only should be grasped clearly and distinctly but also, in so far as possible, should be identified in one's own personal intellectual experience."[4]

Disjunctions Four and Five

The last two disjunctions have to do with the structure of the book. Thomas Aquinas distinguished the order of discovery from the order of teaching. The order of discovery starts with simple and superficial things, pursuing them until finally one comes to the deepest and most basic principles. The order of teaching is the opposite: It begins from the most basic and universal principles, and deduces from them all the intervening realities, until one arrives back at the initial details. In these terms, Lonergan is not following the "order of teaching." He finds it more pedagogical to follow something like the order of discovery.

I remember a chemistry teacher reflecting that God did not create the world to accommodate chemistry 101. There is no simple and logical approach to the body of chemical knowledge; the process is inevitably rather messy. One has to begin somewhere, hopefully with something fairly simple. Then one looks at another area, and another, then comes back possibly to the first area, but sees it at a deeper level. Eventually one wants to tie all the areas together in an integrated vision.

Another helpful image might be of climbing a mountain. On the way, one has partial views, which may indeed be quite stirring, but only at the top does one possess the total view. The earlier views anticipate the full one, but they cannot be used to judge what is to come.

This is what Lonergan means by his "moving viewpoint." The book begins with a small and limited context. Gradually that

---

[4] 14 (xx).

is expanded. But only by about Chapter XV can one begin to see the whole view. Lonergan's caution, then, is that the later view is not to be judged by any prior anticipation of it.

A long disquisition on Gödel's theorem follows. For those totally unfamiliar with modern logic, this may seem mystifying. But it is only a fancy way for Lonergan to reiterate that his interest is only indirectly in the various areas of study (the lower context), and directly and centrally on the act of insight (the upper context).

Finally, Lonergan summarizes the work in a slogan that is worth quoting in full. "*Thoroughly understand what it is to understand, and not only will you understand the broad lines of all there is to be understood but you will also possess a fixed base, an invariant pattern, opening upon all further developments of understanding.*"[5]

Summary

Lonergan offers a first indication of where he is going in the preface and introduction to *Insight*. He points first in the preface to the act of insight; then evokes an insight into insight, working out the implications of this idea in terms of ten aspects and three levels of his book. In the introduction, he formulates his purpose in five disjunctions: statements of what he is *not* doing as well as what he *is* doing.

Questions for Reflection

Are you clear on what Lonergan means by insight? By insight into insight? What do you think is the thrust of the first disjunction, that the question is not the existence but rather the nature of knowledge?

---

[5]22 (xxviii).

Chapter 2

Appropriating Insight Through Examples

READING: *Insight,* Chapter I, pp. 27–46, 55–56
(3–22, 31–32):
A Dramatic Instance; Definition;
Higher Viewpoints; Inverse Insight

As mentioned earlier, the whole first part of *Insight* is concerned with cognitional process, with the question, "What do I do when I know?" To that cognitional process Lonergan sees insight as the key and entry point, and he wastes almost no time in giving some examples of insight. The reader is invited to understand these insights, to have an "insight into insight." But it may be

In the midst of that vast and profound stirring of human minds that was called the Renaissance, Descartes was convinced that too many people felt it beneath them to direct their efforts to apparently trivial problems. Again and again in his *Regulae ad directionem ingenii,* he reverts to this theme. Intellectual mastery of mathematics, of the departments of science, of philosophy is the fruit of a slow and steady accumulation of little insights. Great problems are solved by being broken down into little problems. The strokes of genius are but the outcome of a continuous habit of inquiry that grasps clearly and distinctly all that is involved in the simple things anyone can understand. 27 (3) helpful to the reader to point out that the single insights chosen are only examples. In trying to understand them, there will be many puzzles on the way, and the reader may learn as much about insight by paying attention to what he or she doesn't and does understand, as from the central examples themselves.

Insight One: Archimedes

The first instance Lonergan gives is one of the most famous in all of science: the figure of Archimedes running naked and excited from the baths of Syracuse, yelling "I've got it! I've got it!" We still use the word *eureka* today in similar circumstances.

Lonergan gives rather short shrift to the insight itself, but it may pay to linger on it. What exactly did Archimedes understand, and why was it so momentous? The problem was this: The king had been given a crown by a goldsmith. Assured that it was pure gold, the king still wondered if he was being tricked. So he set the problem for Archimedes: "Find out if this is totally gold, or alloyed with some baser metal. But the crown is too beautiful to damage, so don't harm it in any way."

Two possibilities for deception occur immediately. The crown might be made on a base of some other metal and overlaid with gold. Or perhaps the whole is an alloy like brass, through and through, polished up to look like gold. How would one tell?

A scientist today might use an X-ray machine to discover if there is a discernible boundary between an outer and an inner layer of metal. Or perhaps X-ray crystallography might be used to distinguish the molecular structure of gold from that of brass. But, of course, Archimedes had no X-ray machine so that approach was useless.

One clue might be found in a fact that everyone knows: Some metals are heavier than others. For example, aluminum is relatively light, and lead is relatively heavy. This does not mean, of course, that two pounds of lead are heavier than two pounds of aluminum. It simply means that if one has a piece of lead the same size as a piece of aluminum, the lead will be heavier.

This would not be difficult to quantify. One would take a cubic inch of aluminum and weigh it, and then do the same with the lead. One could also do the same with gold. Then, once one knew the volume of the crown, one could calculate its weight if it were aluminum or lead or gold. If the crown matched the weight for gold, then it was authentic; it if did not, then it was some other metal.

Reflecting on Archimedes

Does the reader understand this so far? Do the insights come easily or more slowly? Catching them "in the act" is what is most important here.

The volume of the crown was tossed off rather lightly. But how does one know that? If the crown has a regular shape, it might be possible to calculate. Suppose the outside of the crown is a sphere, and the inside a smaller sphere. Then one could calculate the two volumes and subtract one from the other. But the crown is likely to be of an irregular shape, with projections here and there. Of course, the crown could be melted down and poured into a standard-sized mold, its volume determined that way. But that violates the king's order not to destroy the crown.

Here the water of Archimedes' bath may come in handy. Imagine a tank of water with an area of 1 foot by 1 foot. Immerse the crown in the water; suppose the water rises one inch. Then the volume of the crown must be 12 x 12 x 1 inch = 144 cubic inches. Given the standard weight of a cubic inch of gold, the proper value could easily be calculated.

In fact, scientists—and this may go back to Archimedes—do not usually weigh a standard quantity, but rather speak of "specific gravity." The specific gravity of a metal is the proportion of its weight to that of an equal quantity of water. The advantage of this system is that it is tied to no specific measure. Imagine a metal with a specific gravity of 15. Then a cubic inch of the metal will weigh 15 times as much as a cubic inch of water, but the same ratio will hold between a quart of the metal and a quart of water, or a gallon of either, or a cubic foot, or a cubic centimeter.

Archimedes' principle, as it is still called, is somewhat more complicated than the above. It holds that an object heavier than water, when submerged, will exhibit an upward buoyancy equal to the weight of the water displaced by the object.

Suppose the crown is placed on a balance beam, and the beam is held level by a 5 pound weight. Now hook a string to the beam and to the crown, and suspend the crown in a tub of water. Will it weigh the same? No, because it is more buoyant in water than it is in air. Suppose the crown now weighs 4 3/4 pounds. That means that there is an upward buoyancy of 1/4 pound, which will be the weight of the water displaced by the crown.

Now fashion a crown in aluminum of the same specifications as the gold one. Say it weighs 2 pounds. When submerged in water, it will weigh 1 3/4 pounds because, having the same volume, it will experience the same upward buoyancy of 1/4 pound. But note the proportions: The 2 pounds of aluminum are related to the 1/4 pound of water as 8 to 1, while the 5 pounds of gold are related to the 1/4 pound of water as 20 to 1. We are back to specific gravity by another path.

The reader is now perhaps in a position to grasp Archimedes' insight. For days he has been racking his brains as to how to meet the king's challenge, to authenticate the crown as pure gold without destroying it. Exhausted by his mental labors, he decides to take a little time off to relax in the baths. As he eases himself into the water, he senses the way his body becomes lighter and more buoyant as he passes from the air into the water. Suddenly the insight hits him: Weigh the crown in the air and then in the water! Implicit in this directive are the principles of specific gravity and displacement of water. He runs from the baths, too excited to stop for his clothes, shouting the good news, "eureka, eureka!"

The solution, brilliant as it is, does seem to overlook one possibility. Suppose the goldsmith was extremely clever and anticipated Archimedes' procedure. Then could he not have combined a heavier and a lighter metal, either in layers, or as an alloy, so that the *average* specific gravity was equal to that of gold? As a matter of fact, gold is heavier than lead, so perhaps that was not a practical worry.

The reader may or may not have been able to follow all of the above. In any case, he will almost certainly have understood some of it. Attention should be directed to those insights. It can hardly be repeated too often that what is paramount here is that the reader grasp the insights taking place in his or her own mind; this is more important than what is going on in Archimedes' or Lonergan's mind.

Characteristics of Insight

Lonergan then goes on to list five characteristics of insight, all of which are nicely illustrated by the story of Archimedes: Insight is the answer to the tension of inquiry; it comes suddenly and unexpectedly, often unpredictably; it is a matter of cognitional, not physical, circumstances; it mediates between the concrete of a particular problem and the abstract principles of specific gravity and displacement; it normally enters into intellectual memory as a permanent possession. All these are relatively straightforward, but, at the risk of overrepetition, the reader should be reminded that the point is to identify those same characteristics in one's own insights, and not just memorize them as Lonergan's pronouncements.

Insight Two: What Makes a Circle?

The second insight Lonergan directs attention to has to do with the definition of a circle. Lonergan is often pointing out that it is one thing to memorize a definition; it is another to understand it, to grasp its inevitability, to see *why* it is defined that way.

A circle is a complete set of points on a flat surface, all equidistant from a center. The circle is a two-dimensional figure; if the surface has bumps or curves, the result will be a three-dimensional figure. Again, the set must be complete, because a half circle or even a shorter arc can have all its points equidistant from a center.

Lonergan begins the search with an image of a bulky wheel. That sets the clue. But in fact, to find the answer, the wheel must be idealized: The rim has to become a line, the spokes infinitely thin and infinitely many, and the hub a point. In the end, one cannot truly imagine the circle, but only think about it.

As the insight mediates between the concrete and the abstract, so it mediates between the image and the thought, or the concept. Without announcing his intentions, Lonergan is here already preparing the reader for the distinction of the two kinds of knowing. A physical wheel can be seen. That same vision can be recaptured or created in imagination. But an infinitely thin line can be neither seen nor imagined. Nor can the "has to," as in, if all the lines are equal, and the rim is but a line, and the center but a point, then the figure *has to* be round. So the physical vision and its imaginative transposition are more the province of sense knowing, while the concept of a line and a point, and the notion of necessity, belong to intellectual knowing.

Gradually Lonergan introduces the accompaniments and the process of insight. As seen already, the image precedes the insight, while the concept follows. But also preceding the insight is the question. It was the question presented by the king that set Archimedes to pondering. It was the question why the wheel was round that led to the understanding of the circle's definition. The

> This primordial drive, then, is the pure question. It is prior to any insights, any concepts, any words; for insights, concepts, words have to do with answers, and before we look for answers we want them; such wanting is the pure question.   34 (9)

question may lead to a clue—not yet the answer, but at least the inkling of it. Imagination plays a role. According to Thomas Aquinas, there is no human understanding without a "phantasm," an image. When all "falls together," the insight has occurred, issuing in a single or multiple concept.

Lonergan next goes on to distinguish nominal, explanatory and implicit definition. If the treatment is not perfectly clear, the issue is a side one, and may be bypassed.

27

Higher Viewpoints

Higher viewpoints, as Lonergan points out in the preface, are crucial to understand, and so some time should be spent on them. An example or two has already been given. In speaking of the structure of a chemistry course, it was pointed out that one begins in a certain place and then perhaps returns to that point in a deeper way. That would be to treat it from a higher viewpoint. Again, there was mention of integrating together a number of areas of chemistry. That would again require a higher viewpoint. In connection with the structure of *Insight,* it was said that Lonergan writes from a "moving viewpoint." As that viewpoint moves from a lesser, more limited context, to one more expansive, the moving viewpoint becomes progressively a higher one. The image of mountain climbing was also presented because it is a good physical metaphor for the intellectual movement to higher and higher viewpoints.

Lonergan chooses a mathematical example. At the risk of finding readers who totally "shut down" intellectually when confronted with mathematical symbols, the point may perhaps be introduced more gently.

As Lonergan shows, all the positive integers can be generated with the simple notions of one, plus and equals. The simplest example is "one plus one equals two." Next, "two plus one equals three." When formulated, this could give the one addition table:

$$1 + 1 = 2$$
$$2 + 1 = 3$$
$$3 + 1 = 4$$
$$4 + 1 = 5$$
$$5 + 1 = 6$$
$$6 + 1 = 7$$
$$7 + 1 = 8$$
$$8 + 1 = 9$$
$$9 + 1 = 10$$

The table for two, three and so on could easily be added. But let us stay with the addition table for one.

Subtraction may then be defined as just the opposite, the undoing of addition.

$$10 - 1 = 9$$
$$9 - 1 = 8$$
$$8 - 1 = 7$$
$$7 - 1 = 6$$
$$6 - 1 = 5$$
$$5 - 1 = 4$$
$$4 - 1 = 3$$
$$3 - 1 = 2$$
$$2 - 1 = 1$$

So far, so good. Comparing the two tables, one can see how subtraction simply undoes what is done in addition. But suppose the process is continued:

$1 - 1 = ?$ There is need for a whole new concept, which is zero. That may seem obvious to us, but it had to be invented by the Arabs: Insight is always easy once it has occurred!

But suppose the process is continued further:

$0 - 1 = ?$ Here still another concept must be added: that of the negative number. Besides the positive integers then, stretching out indefinitely, one must add the zero and negative numbers stretching out indefinitely in the other direction. This requires a higher viewpoint.

Again, the times table was learned in grammar school and is fairly simple; indeed, it is simply a repeated addition. "Three times two" means $2 + 2 + 2 = 6$. So the 2 times table can be constructed:

$$1 \times 2 = 2$$
$$2 \times 2 = 4$$
$$3 \times 2 = 6$$
$$4 \times 2 = 8$$

$5 \times 2 = 10$

$6 \times 2 = 12$

$7 \times 2 = 14$

$8 \times 2 = 16$

$9 \times 2 = 18$

Again, division can be defined as simply the opposite of multiplication:

$18 \div 2 = 9$

$16 \div 2 = 8$

$14 \div 2 = 7$

$12 \div 2 = 6$

$10 \div 2 = 5$

$8 \div 2 = 4$

$6 \div 2 = 3$

$4 \div 2 = 2$

$2 \div 2 = 1$

But suppose that is pursued: $1 \div 2 = ?$ Here one must introduce the notion of the fraction. So besides whole numbers there are fractions; the number system is expanded and a new, higher viewpoint is required.

As can be seen, the higher viewpoints can be cumulative. One starts with a number system of positive integers; then one has a number system of positive integers and zero and negative integers; then a system of positive integers, zero, negative integers and fractions and so on.

Inverse Insight

Finally, in this chapter Lonergan treats of inverse insight, another important notion. When Archimedes headed for the bath, he did not as yet understand. If the reader failed to understand the point of Archimedes' discovery, he did not yet understand. This is a mere failure to understand, the lack of an insight.

Inverse insight is something different from that. In one way, it is positive; something is understood. Yet it is a strange kind of insight, in that it grasps that, in some way, there is nothing to be understood.

There is an old riddle, "What is the difference between a chicken?" The answer is, "Each both has two legs." Clearly, something is amiss here. A difference implies two things to be different. So to ask about the difference of one thing is to ask a poorly formulated question. The appropriate insight is not the supposed answer, which itself is a nonsense phrase, but an understanding that the question makes no sense.

Again, imagine a nonsense song or nursery rhyme in another language. A person might look up all the words in a dictionary and still not make sense of it. Finally, he may ask someone who knows the language, "What does it mean?" That person may answer, "Why, it doesn't mean anything; it's just words." That is an inverse insight: grasping that there is nothing to be understood *where a person would have expected an understanding.*

Or imagine a person used to classical theater who wanders, totally unprepared, into a play of the theater of the absurd. He may at first try to piece together the action in the way he is accustomed to, but he will find the attempt very frustrating. Finally he may come to the insight, "Oh, it's not *expected* to make any sense." That again would be an inverse insight.

Inverse Insight in Science

These examples are relatively trivial, but Lonergan sees a particular importance to inverse insight in physics, so it may be worthwhile to try to understand one of his examples, with apologies again to readers averse to physics.

Our usual experience is that, unless something is continually pushed, it comes to rest. Rest seems like the "natural state" of things; to move something requires an effort, representing an "unnatural state." For example, the car runs only as long as I keep my foot on the accelerator; if I take it off, and kill the motor, the car eventually comes to a stop. The same is true if I skate, or push a wagon, or start someone on a swing: Once no further effort is expended, the motion ends in rest. The obvious question is, "What keeps a thing moving?"

Newton examined this question with a scientist's mentality. As seen already, mathematicians and scientists begin with an image of a rolling wagon or a decelerating car, and try to idealize it. In this case, Newton realized it was friction that made everything slow down and finally stop. But suppose there were no friction. Some examples of that occur in the physical world—if not a perfect lack of friction, at least enough to be suggestive. A car that has well-lubricated bearings will roll further before it finally stops. A puck on an ice-hockey rink will go a great distance with a single shove. A train that is magnetically suspended above a track should be able to go at great speeds with little expenditure of energy for the forward motion. Under conditions of "superconductivity," electrons find little resistance to their passage.

The scientist, then, factors out friction as a distraction. But then an object in motion will tend to move in a straight line forever unless something stops it. Hence, Newton's first law of motion: "...a body continues in its existing state of uniform motion in a straight line unless that state is changed by external force."[1]

So what keeps a thing moving? Contrary to normal commonsense expectations, Newton grasped that there was something wrong with the question. Abstracting from friction, nothing is required to keep a thing moving; rather some intervention is required to *stop* it. So movement is just as natural a state as rest; in fact, rest is simply that special state of movement where the speed is zero. This is an inverse insight and obviously a foundational one in physics.

At this point Lonergan ventures into the history of Aristotelian and Newtonian physics. Unless the reader is particularly interested, this section may be safely ignored. But it might be

------

[1] 46 (21).

worthwhile to read the conclusion of the chapter, beginning on page 55 (31), where Lonergan again reiterates that what is essential is insight into insight, and that the reader is to be encouraged to examine those insights which occur in his or her *own* mind.

Summary

Lonergan tries in Chapter I to give a more accurate idea of insight, appealing first to the historical and scientific insight of Archimedes, and then to a mathematical insight into a circle. He shows how insights can accumulate into higher viewpoints and introduces the inverse insight, the strange type that grasps there is nothing to be grasped.

Questions for Reflection

Formulate in your own words the significance of Archimedes' insight. What five characteristics of insight does it illustrate?

What makes a circle a circle?

What precedes insight? What follows upon it?

Chapter 3

Looking for Insights in
All the Right Places

READING: *Insight,* Chapter II,
pp. 57–62, 91–92 (33–38, 68–69):
Heuristic Structures of Empirical Method

The present guide will try to steer the reader largely around the great amounts of physics and mathematics in the first part of *Insight.* But science is too important to Lonergan's system to avoid entirely, and so some minimum attention must be paid to it in this chapter and the next.

To keep the central focus in mind, however, the main interest of the first part of the book is cognitional process, and especially insight, and the chief insight in question is that taking place in the reader's own head, which may or may not coincide with the examples Lonergan is pointing to.

The Heuristic

Chapter II of *Insight* deals with the *heuristic,* a key term in Lonergan's vocabulary. The word has the same Greek root as Archimedes' *eureka* and means literally to find. More exactly, the term *heuristic* refers to whatever helps in finding an insight. In the last chapter it was stated that the question might give rise to a clue. But how does one find the first clue? The person of common sense often blunders about until he stumbles on it by "accident." Sometimes a cut-and-try method will work: "Let's try a cup of sugar in the recipe; if it turns out too sweet, then we'll reduce it next time." Sometimes a more systematic approach is possible: "It has to be one of these five keys, so let's try them in turn, and see which one works."

But mathematics and science are not so haphazard. Though even there a great deal of blundering may take place, and the great discoveries of science often enough occur by serendipity, nevertheless the mathematician and the scientist have standard procedures that can be called heuristic: They constitute an almost automatic way of generating and utilizing clues. It is partly for this reason that Lonergan focuses so much on mathematical and scientific examples.

Algebra: Looking for an X

> With another bow then to Descartes' insistence on understanding extremely simple things, let us examine the algebraist's peculiar habit of solving problems by announcing, "Let X be the required number." 60 (36)

Lonergan offers an example from algebra. The mathematician has a way of calling an unknown X and then defining the properties of X to derive its value. Lonergan suggests a diagram here, and that might be helpful:

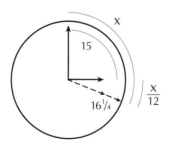

The question is, if the minute hand is at 12, and the hour hand at 3, how many minutes will it take for the minute hand to catch up with the hour hand?

It may be helpful to think in terms of distances. (Of course, the distances are measured by the marks on the clock face, which ultimately represent minutes.) There are three distances involved. The first is the distance the minute hand travels. Call that X. How far will the hour hand travel in the same time? The hour hand travels 5 marks during the time the minute hand makes a complete revolution of 60 marks, so the hour hand travels 5/60 or 1/12 the speed of the minute hand. The hour hand will obviously cover 1/12 of the distance during the time the minute hand covers its distance, X, so the hour hand will cover X/12. But the distance the hour hand covers plus 15 marks is the same as the distance the minute hand covers, X. So

the distance (minute hand) = distance (hour hand) + 15, or
$X = X/12 + 15$.

Multiplying both sides by 12 gives $12 X = X + 180$.

Subtracting X from each side gives $11X = 180$.

Dividing both sides by 11 gives $X = 180/11 = 16\ 4/11$.

So the two hands will meet at the 16 4/11 minute mark.

What Lonergan is particularly interested in here is not so much the mathematics as the notion of the X, the heuristic clue that gets the whole process moving. Again and again the mathematician will follow the same procedure: Draw a diagram, if necessary; name the desired quantity; and relate it to other quantities so that it can be solved for.

Science: Looking for a Nature

The physicist does something similar, but instead of using X, he takes the heuristic beginning to his investigation by asking about the "nature" of whatever he is investigating. Lonergan gives the example of Galileo, who asked: "What is the nature of free fall?" The old Aristotelian doctrine was that the speed of something falling was proportionate to its weight. That was easy enough to disprove: Simultaneously drop two balls of different weights from the Leaning Tower of Pisa, and one can observe that they also hit the ground at the same time.

Another rather obvious fact is that momentum increases over the fall. If one catches a small ball a foot after dropping it, the impact will be minor, but if one catches it after a 50-foot fall, it will make much more of an impression. But how much more? For this answer, Galileo had to experiment. He rolled balls down inclined planes and dropped balls off high places. Eventually, he had enough data to conclude that the distance traversed increased as the square of the time. This means that the speed also increases with time.

As a matter of fact, if something drops from an airplane, it does not speed up indefinitely. At a certain point the air resistance prevents it from speeding up any more; it reaches its "terminal velocity." But, as Newton abstracted from friction in formulating his first law of motion, so Galileo followed this scientific habit in formulating his law of falling bodies, presuming that they were falling in a perfect vacuum. That is an ideal state, of course, which can be approximated physically, but never fully achieved. But the scientist is more interested in conceptual precision.

Mathematics and science are alike, then, in that both have heuristic procedures; the mathematician asks, "What is X?" while the scientist asks, "What is the nature of...?" But, as Lonergan points out, there are also key differences between the two fields. The mathematician can work in his study, at most drawing a diagram. But the physicist must get out into the field and experiment, must climb the Leaning Tower of Pisa and drop the balls and time their descent.

In understanding the definition of the circle, reference was made to a certain "has to." But in science there is no similar necessity. The physicist investigates not how the world has to be, but how in fact it is. That marks the largest difference between the older Aristotelian science and the newer, modern one. Aristotelian science was deductive, while modern science is inductive.

As Lonergan moves into differential equations, we will tip-toe politely away. But the reader may find helpful the survey beginning on page 91(68). Periodically, Lonergan will pause to summarize what has been covered and announce what will be coming; these periodic surveys of past and future progress will help the reader keep his bearings. Once again Lonergan reiterates that what is being investigated is the "concrete, individual, existing subject": that is, the reader, with his or her own cognitional process.

Summary

People not only have insights, Lonergan points out in Chapter II, but they also actively seek insights. However, what a person of common sense does spontaneously, the mathematician and the scientist do systematically and methodically, saying, "Let X be the required number" or asking, "What is the nature of...?"

Questions for Reflection

What, in your own words, does "heuristic" mean?
Why is the mathematician always looking for X?
What is the significance of the scientist's search for a nature?

Chapter 4

What Does Science Know About Knowing?

READING: None

Chapter III of *Insight* plunges almost immediately into rather deep waters. In spite of his protestations that "our aim is still into the nature of insight," and "...our interest...is...exhibiting still more clearly and convincingly the fact and nature of insight,"[1] it does appear that Lonergan here is making his own stab at an account of scientific method; he is also presuming matters already skipped over in this commentary. Nevertheless, it may be worthwhile to spend a little more time on the subject of science before moving on, making occasional reference to early pages of this chapter.

The Nature of Empirical Science

Lonergan points out on page 96 (73), for example, that sense presentations emerge within a context of interest. I took a walk in the woods with a naturalist. He was constantly pointing out plants, birds and animals I would have completely overlooked. Were his eyes better than mine? Not necessarily. He was simply more habituated to look for the flora and fauna than I was. One evening, more recently, I was riding in a van with a cousin at dusk. A

---

[1] 94 (71).

Before undertaking a fuller account of these canons, it may not be amiss to recall our viewpoint and purpose. The reader must not expect us to retell the history of the development of empirical method, nor look for descriptive accounts of what scientists do, nor anticipate an argument based on the authority of great names in science, nor hope for a summary of directives, precepts, and recipes to guide him in the practice of scientific investigation. Our aim still is an insight into the nature of insight. Our presumption is that empirical investigators are intelligent. Our supposition will be that the reader is already sufficiently familiar with scientific history and procedures, authoritative pronouncements and practical directives. Our single purpose is to reveal the intelligible unity that underlies and accounts for the diverse and apparently disconnected rules of empirical method. Our concern is not what is done, or how it is done, but why. And our interest in seeking the reason why is not to extend methodology but to unify it, not to unify it so that methodology may be improved, but rather to unify it in the hope of exhibiting still more clearly and convincingly the fact and the nature of insight.   94 (70–71)

deer-hunter himself, he pointed out the deer in a field, which I could hardly distinguish when I looked as closely as possible. I once had a similar, more prosaic experience. Over a few weekends I took on as a project searching in ditches for aluminum cans. For some time afterward, wherever I would go, the aluminum cans would pop out at me—not a very aesthetic way of viewing a landscape! Knowing begins in the senses, then, yet they already exhibit an orientation geared to the interests and the habits of the person employing them.

Science by its nature, Lonergan further asserts, is limited to sense data.[2] Does a human being have a soul? Do angels exist? Did God create the universe? These questions go beyond the competence of the scientist because they escape the realm of sense data. Nevertheless, Lonergan holds, to say that something cannot be

[2] 95–96 (72).

known by science is not to say it cannot be known at all.[3] There may be other, perfectly valid ways of knowing, whose evidence does not depend on direct sense experience.

In fact, Lonergan points out, there can be more than one kind of experience. Besides the sense experience, familiar to everyone, there is also the experience of the mental process itself.[4] As already mentioned, everyone has a private and privileged access to his own mental operations. Lonergan is hinting here that just as a physical science is built on sense data, so a mental science, a "generalized empirical method," could be built upon the data of consciousness. This is a suggestion Lonergan will pursue later in the book.

Science and Common Sense

Lonergan also makes a distinction between the relation of things to us, and to each other.[5] This is a crucial distinction for him. To understand it, return to the differing orientations of sense experience already mentioned. The contrast Lonergan is pointing to is that between the man of common sense and the scientist. He mentions as an example Thales and the milkmaids.[6] Thales was a Greek astronomer, absorbed in studying the stars. A group of milkmaids, practical women, are watching him. As he walks about, his gaze raised raptly to the night sky, he suddenly falls into a well! The milkmaids laugh—how could anyone be so dumb as not to watch where he was going? Simple as it is, the story illustrates two different orientations. Both the milkmaids and Thales have eyes and can see both the stars and the ground. The milkmaids, however, fix their eyes on the ground, taking the stars for granted. Both the milkmaids and Thales had human minds and could wonder, but it is only Thales who fixes that wonder on the stars.

The milkmaids are practical people, who are merely concerned about getting their work done, about walking from the house to the barn without falling into the well. But Thales wonders

---

[3] 95 (72).
[4] 96 (72).
[5] 97, 101–2 (73, 78–79).
[6] 96 (73).

how things are, what paths the stars and planets follow, what influence they might have on human affairs, a knowledge that is not, at least immediately, practical—so impractical, in fact, that he falls into a well!

The person of common sense is satisfied with ordinary experience: "It feels cold tonight. I'll wear a sweater so as not to catch a cold." But such feelings are notoriously subjective. What feels cold to one person may seem quite warm to another. The scientist is interested in something more objective. Eventually he will invent a thermometer, which any two people can read to get the same temperature. Hot and cold, then, are no longer related to us, but to gradations on a column of mercury.

Common sense, again, is geographically limited. In a place where there are no wells, the practical wisdom of not falling into them may be irrelevant. Perhaps knowing how not to step on rattlesnakes might be more helpful. But the scientist is looking for something more universal. He wants a science that will be as valid in Topeka, Kansas, as in Greenwich, England. Otherwise, a science would have to be worked out for each particular place, and the worldwide collaboration of scientists would collapse.

"Hence, to become a scientific observer is, not to put an end to perception, but to bring the raw materials of one's sensations within a new context. The interests and hopes, desires and fears, of ordinary living have to slip into a background. In their place, the detached and disinterested exigences of inquiring intelligence have to enter and assume control."[7] Lonergan is here intimating another idea important to his analysis of cognition: the drive to know. It is the initial wonder that sparks inquiry, the tension that keeps the scientist at work, the motive spring from which all intellectual process takes its dynamism. The person of common sense knows to live, but in the scientist knowing becomes a quest of knowledge for its own sake; faithful to the austere but powerful drive to know, the scientist lives to know.

---

[7]93 (73).

What Science Tells Us About Knowing

Why does Lonergan devote so much of *Insight* to scientific knowing? It is because modern science has, in its own development, been forced into a discovery about knowing. Euclid worked out his geometry over two thousand years ago. It all seemed so simple and so obvious; for century upon century people just assumed this geometry represented the way the universe was.

But then some mathematicians in the nineteenth century began experimenting with Euclid's postulates. One of his assumptions is that two parallel lines, extended indefinitely, will never meet. Suppose, one mathematician said, parallel lines *do* eventually meet. Could a geometry be worked out with that assumption? It appeared it could—and one just as rigorous and logical as Euclid's. Suppose, another mathematician said, the lines kept diverging further and further as they are extended. Could that assumption ground a valid geometry? Indeed it could and, once again, one quite as rigorous and logical as Euclid's.

Still, this remained an intellectual curiosity. People continued to presume that Euclid's was the geometry for the real world, while the others were mere mathematical extravagances. But in the twentieth century something strange happened: Einstein proposed that space was curved. Thus, it was not Euclid's, but one of the alternative geometries, that truly mapped the universe!

This is very difficult to imagine. It goes against all the spontaneous anticipations that Euclid's is, of course, the correct geometry and suggests that imagination is not a safe guide to the structure of the universe, that scientific knowing has entered into a realm no longer accessible to the imagination.

This intimation was further verified in the twentieth century. Quantum mechanics presented something called a *wavicle,* which had some characteristics of a wave and some of a particle. Of course, this is impossible to visualize. The scientist must retire into mathematical equations to describe it. But the upshot, once again, is that scientific knowing has broken with imagination.

For Lonergan, then, the developments of recent science have indicated the complexity of human knowing. Knowing is not simply looking with the eyes, nor is it even picturing with the imagination. Insight gives access to a level of thought that takes its start in, but then transcends, sense and imagination. Paradoxically science, focused on sense data, has gradually revealed that human knowing must be more than mere sense data.

Summary

Lonergan continues to explore science in his third chapter. Three aspects are singled out here: Science is empirical, based on sense experience; science is a form of knowing quite distinct from common sense; and twentieth-century science has made key discoveries about human knowing.

Questions for Reflection

Do we experience the knowing process itself? Is that a part of empirical science?

Do you tend to be more a commonsense or a scientific person?

What exactly does contemporary science tell us about the process of knowing?

Chapter 5

Let's Use Some Common Sense!

READING: *Insight*, Chapter VI, pp. 196–212 (173–89):
Common Sense as Intellectual;
the Subjective Field of Common Sense

With Chapter VI, Lonergan shifts gears in a marked way. From heady matters of science and mathematics, he returns to the concrete world of common sense. As before, however, the unifying theme is insight. Sometimes insight is identified with the major breakthroughs of science. But insight plays a role as well in more prosaic ways.

> ...one meets intelligence in every walk of life. There are intelligent farmers and craftsmen, intelligent employers and workers, intelligent technicians and mechanics, intelligent doctors and lawyers, intelligent politicians and diplomats. There is intelligence in industry and commerce, in finance and taxation, in journalism and public relations. There is intelligence in the home and in friendship, in conversation and in sport, in the arts and in entertainment. In every case, the man or woman of intelligence is marked by a greater readiness in catching on, in getting the point, in seeing the issue, in grasping implications, in acquiring know-how. In their speech and action the same characteristics can be discerned, as were set forth in describing the act that released Archimedes' "Eureka."[1]

---

[1] 196 (173).

Retrospect

Lonergan has given various examples of insight. He has also shown how inquiry is started by a question. The question creates a state of tension, which is only broken by the occurrence of the desired insight. Lonergan has also shown how the movement from question to insight is not left to chance, but is itself intelligent. The search for insight is heuristic, the work of active, inquiring intelligence. Obviously, the questioning mind does not know the answer, or the search would already be terminated. Yet there are anticipations of the answer; some clues appear more likely than others, some imaginative pictures more helpful than others. In mathematics and science, these heuristic anticipations are routinized and systematized: What is X? What is the nature of...?

Insight also, it was seen, presumes a prior level of presentations. This is ordinarily given by the senses, perhaps recombined in the imagination. Insight is an understanding, but there must be something to understand. In the first instance, this is the deliverance of the senses. Sense experience is not the full tally of human knowing, yet knowing always begins in sense.

Lonergan has also pointed out that though insight is of a piece, yet it occurs in many different areas or in characteristic patterns. A further analysis of those patterns is the central issue of the first part of Chapter VI. The initial contrast is between scientific and commonsense knowing. Having examined scientific knowing, he can now use it as a foil to compare and contrast commonsense knowing.

Scientific and Common Sense Contrasted

Lonergan points out eight contrasts between scientific and commonsense knowing. First, science is methodical, whereas commonsense knowing is spontaneous. Scientific method is a cornerstone of science; the scientist lives and dies by his method. But in the world of common sense, spontaneity rules. A child does not have to be taught to ask questions; it happens naturally, sometimes to the point of parents' distraction. At first, the search is

The light and drive of intelligent inquiry unfolds methodically in mathematics and empirical science. In the human child it is a secret wonder that, once the mystery of language has been unraveled, rushes forth in a cascade of questions. Far too soon the questions get out of hand, and weary adults are driven to ever more frequent use of the blanket "My dear, you cannot understand that yet." The child would like to understand everything at once. It does not suspect that there is a strategy in the accumulation of insights, that the answers to many questions depend on answers to still other questions, that often enough advertence to these other questions arises only from the insight that to meet interesting questions one has to begin from quite uninteresting ones. There is, then, common to all men the very spirit of inquiry that constitutes the scientific attitude. But in its native state it is untutored. Our intellectual careers begin to bud in the incessant what and why of childhood. They flower only if we are willing, or constrained, to learn how to learn. They bring forth fruit only after the discovery that, if we really would master the answers, we somehow have to find them out ourselves. 196–97 (173–74)

distinctly UNmethodical: The child wants to know everything at once. Only gradually does inquiring intelligence realize there is a strategy to knowing: Some things must be learned as a basis for others. Some are tools, tedious, perhaps, but necessary to know many other things.

Moreover, insights are not isolated instances. Spontaneously, inquiring intelligence is at work integrating and relating them. Insights on a particular topic assimilate to each other, eventually making a rounded whole: the mastery of one field.

Again, insights are not merely the work of individuals. Knowing is a human collaboration. A person with an insight spontaneously wishes to share it with another. "Let me tell you what I found out!" Teachers do it more formally in the classroom, but parents, siblings, friends, neighbors may be at it in practically any conversation. Knowing the insight already, it is as if a path has been trod; the learner walks in the footsteps of the knower, who points out the landmarks to follow, the obstacles and snares to avoid.

Lonergan mentions on page 198 (175) the "self-correcting process of knowing," an idea important to his thought. Not only do questions and insights spontaneously arise; not only do they coalesce by a natural attraction; not only do people spontaneously lead others to insight, but inquiring intelligence is also continually correcting its mistakes, and learning from them. A new insight seems to challenge an old one—which is correct? One acts on a new insight and the action fails—was there perhaps something wrong in the first place? The human mind is not infallible; it can make mistakes—but it is also intelligently aware of that fact, alert to its occurrence and intelligently able to correct its errors.

Further Contrasts

Second, scientific knowing quickly develops a technical jargon. Geometry, as mentioned already, formulates a series of postulates. But common sense has no use for such a logical

Common sense, on the other hand, never aspires to universally valid knowledge, and it never attempts exhaustive communication. Its concern is the concrete and particular. Its function is to master each situation as it arises. Its procedure is to reach an incomplete set of insights that is to be completed only by adding on each occasion the further insights that scrutiny of the occasion reveals. It would be an error for common sense to attempt to formulate its incomplete set of insights in definitions and postulates and to work out their presuppositions and implications. For the incomplete set is not the understanding either of any concrete situation or of any general truth. Equally, it would be an error for common sense to attempt a systematic formulation of its completed set of insights in some particular case; for every systematic formulation envisages the universal, and every concrete situation is particular. 200 (176–77).

panoply. Rather than habitually defining words in a very precise way, it has a ready and shrewd grasp of their range of possible meanings.

Third, scientific knowing searches for principles and laws; its ultimate goal is a complete explanation of the universe. But the ambitions of common sense are much more modest. It operates with proverbs—pithy sayings that indicate a mode of action, but always with the proviso: all things being equal. All things being equal, the early bird gets the worm. But all things being equal, it is better to be safe than sorry. But when are all things equal? A prudential judgment is necessary in each case to mate the situation with its appropriate proverb, and so the wisdom of common sense remains incomplete, ready to be applied, when the situation arises, only by a further prudential insight.

Fourth, scientific knowing tries to be exhaustive. It wants to know everything and state accurately and completely all it knows. But common sense is content to say only what is needed for the moment. Polonius, trying to communicate to Laertes all the common sense he has collected, tends to make of himself a fool. A word to the wise is sufficient!

Fifth, science aims at the universal, while common sense clings to the particular. Science wants to be valid everywhere, but the shoemaker sticks to his last, and the commonsense knower to cultivating his own garden, little concerned about how people do things elsewhere.

Sixth, science wants to relate things to each other, while common sense is satisfied to remain in the world of things-as-related-to-us. This thought was already introduced in the last chapter of the commentary.[2] Like everyone else, of course, the scientist begins with the feel and touch of things, but quickly he wants to use these first approximations to move on to a more objective and universal kind of measurement.

Seventh, science has theoretical aspirations. It wishes to make an abstract statement about things-as-related-to-each-other. But common sense has no such ambitions; it is determinedly,

---

[2]See above, p. 41.

sometimes almost aggressively, practical. What do all your scientific musings have to do with the price of cabbage?

Eighth, science moves sooner, rather than later, into a very recondite and unfamiliar world. In popular imagination, only a few people in the whole world really understood what Einstein was talking about! But common sense is content to remain in the world of the familiar. Down-home cooking will do very nicely, thank you!

Specificity of Common Sense

These contrasts of science and common sense, Lonergan goes on to say, produce a peculiar characteristic of common sense. Precisely because it is not universal, because it clings to the particular and familiar, it must vary from place to place, and, even more, from time to time. For what is familiar in one place may be quite unfamiliar in another. The particulars of one era will vary from those of another, and so common sense is all but useless except in its specific place and its particular time. Hence common sense must be differentiated for each situation. The immigrant who moves to another country is faced with the task of gradually assembling a largely new fund of common sense.

I remember vividly my first evening in Japan. My host took me to the airport restaurant. Naturally, white rice was served with the meal, but I did not know as yet the almost mystical feeling the Japanese have for white rice. I had only eaten rice with gravy, so I took the bottle of soy sauce and began to douse the rice with it. "Behave yourself!" my Japanese host sharply reproved.

Patterns of Experience

Next, Lonergan goes on to expand his analysis. Insight takes place in many patterns, and Lonergan considers four. The first is the biological pattern. As already noted, man is the *animal rationalis*, and so we have much in common with the animals whose senses are oriented outward: toward game to pursue or enemies or dangers to avoid. Humans share something of the same spontaneous orientation to the outer world that Lonergan terms *extroversion*. Still, it is rare that a human being is in a merely biological state. Perhaps when one is lying on the beach, half awake, half dozing, feeling the wind and the sun, hearing the waves, without a thought in mind or a care in the world, such a purely biological experience exists. But at almost any other time questions are arising, inquiring intelligence is about its busy work, insights occur to make the surroundings fall into intelligible place. In the purely biological pattern, of course, no insights take place.

Second is the aesthetic pattern of experience. Unlike the commonsense pattern, and more like the scientific, the concern here is more contemplative than active; the experience is valued for its own sake and not for some utilitarian purpose. But unlike the scientific pattern, art has no theoretical aspirations. Like the commonsense mode, it clings more to the particular. It wants to understand, but in *these* images and *this* particular situation, with *these* accompanying feelings and *this* particular mood. It is also this particularized insight that the artist wants to communicate. The artist has an insight, then, but it so clings to the particular and concrete that he or she communicates it, not by a universal concept, but through this particular performance or work of art.

Third is the intellectual pattern of experience, which is largely coincident with the scientific pattern already described. In the intellectual pattern, the pure desire to know is set free and is given its own head to establish its own goals. Knowing is no longer for the practical purpose of getting something done, but for the larger end of knowing itself. Lonergan gives a certain priority to intellectual knowing. Only there do things appear as they truly are; by contrast, commonsense knowing is burdened by a bias because it refuses to examine the long-term, abstract and theoretical implications of its positions and judgments.

Fourth is what Lonergan calls the dramatic or the dramatico-practical pattern of experience. It will again be recognized as largely coincident with the commonsense pattern already explored, except that here Lonergan is imagining the individual commonsense knower as the actor in a drama: All the world's a stage! Here, too, insight is active and influential:

> As other insights emerge and accumulate, so too do the insights that govern the imaginative projects of dramatic living. As other insights are corrected through the trial and error that give rise to further questions and yield still further complementary insights, so too does each individual discover and develop the possible roles he might play and, under the pressure of artistic and affective criteria, work out his own selection and adaptation.[3]

Summary

The humbler world of common sense, often neglected by philosophers, is Lonergan's topic in Chapters VI and VII. Though not aspiring to the heights of mathematical or scientific brilliance, it is no less insightful. Lonergan first points out eight contrasts between scientific and commonsense knowing. Then he expands the viewpoint to consider four modes of inner experience: biological, aesthetic, scientific and common sense. Lonergan places a premium on the intellectual or scientific pattern.

Questions for Reflection

What do scientists typically think of commonsense knowing?

What do people of common sense typically think of scientific knowing?

In which pattern of experience do you spend the bulk of your time?

---

[3] 211–12 (188).

Chapter 6

The Jekyll and Hyde
of Human Knowing

READING: *Insight,* Chapter VIII,
pp. 270–79, 292–95 (245–54, 267–70):
"Things" and "Bodies"

In the treatment of the first disjunction of Lonergan's introduction,[1] it was noted that for him the principal question is not whether knowledge exists, but how its two basic kinds can be differentiated and distinguished. In his treatment of the "thing"[2] and the "body"[3] he returns to this theme.

A Note on Terms

An opening word on terminology is necessary. Much later in the book Lonergan reveals that the "thing" is really Aristotelian substance,[4] but that he has avoided this term because of the massive confusions "substance" has been subjected to in modern philosophy. One may sympathize with Lonergan's dilemma, but "thing" is altogether too undifferentiated a word to serve as a

---

[1]See above, p. 17.
[2]270 (245).
[3]275 (250).
[4]462 (436)

good substitute. It would seem better to retain the original word and attempt by explanation to avoid the misunderstanding.

Modern philosophy, beginning with Descartes, has always been closely related to modern science. But science, as seen already, is limited to the data of sense.[5] Hence modern philosophy has exhibited a pervasive temptation to empiricism. If everything can be known by sense, the substance must be knowable by sense. *Substance* means literally to *stand under*. So modern philosophy pictured substance as somehow standing under the appearances of things. If the scientist dug deep enough, he could reach it. Of course, substance was never found by the scientist and so was ridiculed by the philosopher.

But science itself, as noted already, has paradoxically revealed that there is more to human knowing than sense experience and imagination.[6] So it is time to rehabilitate the notion of substance. In this commentary "thing" and "body" will be used sparingly; "substance" and "accident" will be retained; "reality" and "appearances" will also be used at times as substitutes.

What Is a "Thing"?

To return from this digression on terminology, what exactly does Lonergan mean by "thing" and "body"? "All that glitters is not gold" the saying goes. What this proverb warns is that appearances do not always coincide with reality. There is a pyrite that is called *fool's gold*. At first sight, it may appear to be gold, but further tests—perhaps of its specific gravity—reveal that it is counterfeit.

Another proverb appears to run in the other direction. "If it walks like a duck, and quacks like a duck, then it must *be* a duck." This brings out the close connection between the appearance of something and its reality. But, like most proverbs, it is not infallible. Possibly someone could build a robot that convincingly walks like a duck and quacks like a duck, yet it

---

[5]See above, p. 40.
[6]See above, pp. 43–44.

would not be a duck. Those examples are first approximations. What Lonergan means by "thing" is a reality as the object

> Now the notion of a thing is grounded in an insight that grasps, not relations between data, but a unity, identity, whole in data. This unity is grasped, not by considering data from any abstractive viewpoint, but by taking them in their concrete individuality and in the totality of their aspects. For if the reader will turn his mind to any object he names as a thing, he will find that object to be a unity to which belongs every aspect of every datum within the unity. Thus, the dog Fido is a unity, and to Fido is ascribed a totality of data whether of color or shape, sound or odor, feeling or movement. Moreover, from this grasp of unity in a concrete totality of data there follow the various characteristics of things. 271 (246)

of thought, what is expressed by the concept *gold* or *duck*. The concept presumes a prior insight into the nature of gold or the duck.

Distinction from "Body"

The "body," on the other hand, is the reality as apprehended by the senses. It is the appearances of the gold or the duck, what is seen, heard, touched, smelled and tasted of them. In other words, the "body" is what can be grasped by any other animal; it is the object of the animal extroversion mentioned in the last chapter.[7] The "thing" or the substance, by contrast, is not apprehended as such by other animals; only human knowers have insights and concepts.

But often, Lonergan avers, thing is confused with body, substance with its accidents or appearances. Then human knowing

---

[7]See above, p. 51.

collapses into animal or sense knowing, and great philosophical mischief results.

As in the previous chapters, insight remains the focus. The thing is also known by an insight, as already seen, but it is a different kind of insight. Many insights in science are grasps of relations: the relation of time to distance in a falling body, for example. But what is it that moves over distance as the time passes? It is the falling body itself. Rather than an individual aspect, then, the substance is the "unity-identity-whole" in the data. It is the subject to which movement over distance and through time is ascribed or attributed.

Substance and Science

The notion of substance, then, is unavoidably presumed by science. For if there is no falling body, how can there be a distance it traverses or a time which that takes? Similarly, the notion of substance is necessary for the idea of change, which is recognized when the one reality has such-and-such appearances at one time and different appearances at another. Without the underlying unity of substance, there would be simply the elimination of one appearance and the creation of another.

Further, substances appear as particular, yet similar kinds of things occur. "Duck" is not merely the individual living thing here before me, but rather denotes a universal concept, expressing the nature of all ducks. Again, science is dependent on this notion of universal substance; if there had to be a separate science for each duck and each mosquito, then science would never get very far.

In closing this section, Lonergan returns to the epistemological implications of modern science.[8] A tree may be sensed or it may be thought; it may be a body or a thing, sensed in its appearances or thought in its substance. Yet an electron can be thought, but it cannot be sensed; it cannot be apprehended as a body but

---

[8] 275 (250).

only thought as a substance. Thus, modern science has forced a distinction between the appearance and the substance.

Before leaving this section, it should be noted that Lonergan distinguishes two kinds of questions: questions for intelligence, and questions for reflection.[9] This will lead directly to the topic of the next chapter, judgment.

What Is a "Body"?

When he comes to explaining more fully the notion of *body*, Lonergan cites the example of the kitten.[10] Body or appearance, then, is what is encountered in the pattern of purely biological consciousness; it is the object of sense extroversion. Lonergan regularly refers to this as the "already out there now real." As already mentioned, much of modern philosophy tends to be empiricist, and Lonergan details the confusion of thing and body, substance and appearance, in modern thought.[11]

Lonergan goes on to contrast the two kinds of knowing. He cautions that it is not a matter of eliminating one kind, but of critically distinguishing them. He formulates these conclusions on pages 278–79 (253–54).

At the end of the chapter Lonergan again offers a concluding summary, which may be of some help in orienting the beginning reader. "Accordingly, our first task was to clarify the nature of insight, and to it we devoted the first five chapters."[12] But in the course of that investigation the role of a level of presentations, of sense data and imagination, was also revealed. Further, the level of sense experience, and its prolongation in imagination, was sharply distinguished from a level of question, insight and conception. On that basis, thing and body could be distinguished: the substance grasped only on the level of thought, the appearances encountered on the level of sense extroversion. Lonergan goes on to point out[13]

---

[9]273 (248).
[10]276 (251).
[11]277 (252).
[12]293 (267).
[13]293 (268)

The problem set by the two types of knowing is, then, not a problem of elimination but a problem of critical distinction. For the difficulty lies, not in either type of knowing by itself, but in the confusion that arises when one shifts unconsciously from one type to the other. Animals have no epistemological problems. Neither do scientists, as long as they stick to their task of observing, forming hypotheses and verifying. The perennial source of nonsense is that, after the scientist has verified his hypothesis, he is likely to go a little further and tell the layman what, approximately, scientific reality looks like! Already we have attacked the unverifiable image, but now we can see the origin of the strange urge to foist upon mankind unverifiable images. For both the scientist and the layman, besides being intelligent and reasonable, also are animals. To them as animals, a verified hypothesis is just a jumble of words or symbols. What they want is an elementary knowing of the "really real," if not through sense, at least by imagination.   278 (253)

that this is an accomplishment within the intellectual pattern of experience. When one withdraws from that pattern, one is very likely again to fall into the confusion of thing with body, of substance with its appearances. Here emerges, as already mentioned,[14] the priority Lonergan accords to the intellectual pattern. "Accordingly, the attainment of a critical position means not merely that one distinguishes clearly between things and 'bodies' but also that one distinguishes between the different patterns of one's own experience and refuses to commit oneself intellectually unless one is operating within the intellectual pattern of experience."[15]

In closing, he refers again to the second kind of question, the critical "Is it so?" that will be the subject of the next chapter.

---

[14]See above, pp. 51–52.
[15]293 (268).

Summary

Lonergan, up to Chapter VIII, has spoken mostly of relations. Now the time has come to ask: What is it that is related? What *has* the relations? The answer is the substance, what Lonergan calls the *thing*. Substance, too, is known by insight. But, whereas relations are abstract, the substance is the individual concrete existent, so a different kind of insight is required, one that grasps the "unity-identity-whole."

But human beings are animals as well as thinkers; besides having insights, they also have sense encounters with things, much as animals do. A great task of sound philosophy, Lonergan avers, is to distinguish and keep straight that mental grasp and that sense encounter: to distinguish substance or thing from sense appearance or body.

Questions for Reflection

Why do you think that Lonergan has waited so long to introduce the basic notion of the thing?

What does Kant say about our knowledge of things and bodies?

Chapter 7

You Have to Be Judgmental!

READING: *Insight,* Chapter IX, pp. 296–303 (271–78):
The Notion of Judgment

In this chapter Lonergan introduces judgment, which is, along with insight, one of the key elements of his analysis of cognitional process. In fact, it is often this element of judgment that Lonergan finds to differentiate himself most specifically from the majority of modern philosophers. For Descartes, the criterion of truth is the clear and distinct idea.

> And having remarked that there was nothing at all in the statement "I think, therefore I am" which assures me of having thereby made a true assertion, excepting that I see very clearly that to think it is necessary to be, I come to the conclusion that I might assume, as a general rule, that the things which we conceive very clearly and distinctly are all true....[1]

Kant is very clear on the role of sense and the role of the concept in knowing. In a famous summary statement he says, "Thoughts without content are empty; intuitions without

[1]René Descartes, *Discourse on the Method of Rightly Conducting the Reason,* in E. Haldane and G. Ross (tr.), *The Philosophical Works of Descartes,* 2 volumes (Cambridge, England: University Press, 1968–1970), volume 1, p. 102.

concepts are blind."[2] But he does not put the central emphasis on judgment that Lonergan does.

The Reflective Question

As already anticipated and here made clearer, Lonergan distinguishes two kinds of questions. One is for information; it is already familiar as the question that leads to an insight. The answer to this question is a number in arithmetic, a correlation of measurements in physics, or the name of a "unity-identity-whole" in common sense. To this kind of question a simple *Yes* or *No* answer would be meaningless.

But insight is not merely preceded by a question; it is also regularly *followed* by a question. Is it so? Is that true? Are you sure? This is the question for reflection. Insight, then, is revealed by the question for reflection as less than the whole story of human knowing. Rather, it is in the nature of a hypothesis that must still be verified.

In mathematics, this is a process known as checking. Suppose one number is subtracted from another. The question arises: "Is the result correct?" The mathematician usually answers the question by reversing the process. Add the result to the subtrahend; it should give the original minuend. If it doesn't, one goes back to see where the mistake was made.

Science, ever aware of its method, has also formulated this process. The insight is known technically as a hypothesis. It represents a possible correlation of the data. But the scientist is not content to stop with the hypothesis. He asks: "Is it true?" To answer that question, he designs a crucial experiment. If the hypothesis is true, this should be the result; if the hypothesis is false, then the opposite should be the result. If the hypothesis is consistently verified, then it is on its way to becoming a theory or law; if it is falsified, the scientist has to go back to the data, and form a new hypothesis, by having a new insight.

Common sense has no such explicit method. Yet it too has its own shrewd ways to put the question for reflection and withhold

---

[2]Immanuel Kant, *Critique of Pure Reason*, tr. N. Smith (New York: St. Martin's Press, 1965, © 1929), B75, p. 93.

judgment until the evidence is in. "Are you sure you know what you're talking about?" a person may be challenged. "Where's your evidence?" the objector may persist. "Let's not make a judgment until all the facts are in," another person may warn. Common sense as well, then, knows that insight is hypothetical, grasping a possible relation or pattern, but the insight must be checked, and its clear evidence produced, before it can be definitively accepted.

The Finality of Judgment

The possibility of withholding judgment is connected with another aspect of judging: It is a personal commitment. Even common sense knows there is such a thing as a "rush to judgment," and recognizes as well that this violates good cognitional process. This process reaches a high degree of formality in the world of

A third determination of the notion of judgment is that it involves a personal commitment. As de la Rochefoucauld remarked, "Everyone complains of his memory but no one of his judgment." One is ready to confess to a poor memory because one believes that memory is not within one's power. One is not ready to confess to poor judgment because the question for reflection can be answered not only by *Yes* or *No* but also by "I don't know"; it can be answered assertorically or modally, with certitude, or only probability; finally, the question as presented can be dismissed, distinctions introduced and new questions substituted. The variety of possible answers makes full allowance for the misfortunes and shortcomings of the person answering, and by the same stroke it closes the door on possible excuses for mistakes. A judgment is the responsibility of the one that judges. It is a personal commitment.   297 (272)

publishing, where lawyers peruse a proposed article or book to make sure the publisher cannot be held liable for a rash judgment. Once a judgment is published, and it turns out to be false, a person who is harmed by the lie may sue the publisher for defamation, especially if he can prove the false judgment was issued knowingly and maliciously.

Judgment, then, has a certain finality about it. It puts paid to one episode of knowing; it is the "total increment in human knowing."[3] That does not mean, of course, that human knowing comes to an end, but only that it must strike out on a new course, with new data, or new insight, to arrive at a further judgment.

Knowing, then, can be thought of as the sum total of one's judgments. Any one judgment, consequently, is complexly related to others. A new judgment may contradict an old one. Then an inquiry must establish which of the two judgments is false. If it is not contradictory, then the new judgment must be integrated with those already possessed.

Usually we can concentrate on only one judgment at a time, though it may be comprehensive, integrating and organizing a great number of partial judgments. But most of human knowing inevitably remains habitual. It is present somehow in memory and can be recalled, but all our judgments cannot be recalled at once. God's knowing is simultaneous, all at once; human knowing is irretrievably habitual, progressing one judgment at a time, which itself will be committed to intellectual memory as we pursue the next question.

The Structure of Human Knowing

Given the finality of judgment, Lonergan has come to the end of his cognitional analysis, which is summarized in the chart on page 299 (274). This analysis has revealed three major levels: presentations, intelligence and reflection. Because Lonergan often speaks of insight as a second level transcending sense data, and judgment as a third level transcending insight, the three levels may be represented in reverse order.

Level of reflection	(Judgment)
Level of intelligence	(Insight)
Level of presentations	(Sense data)

---

[3] 301 (276).

Further, each of these levels, as already seen, has more than one component; insight and judgment are only the central activities on the second and third levels. So, on the level of presentations, knowing begins in the senses, but it is prolonged in the imagination. The imagination allows a memory of a sense datum no longer present to the knower. Moreover, the imagination can also combine elements given in sense in new ways, to create pictures of things never actually experienced. Still further, it was noted that experience is not merely of the world around us, through the senses; there is also an experience of an "inner world" to which each human knower has a personal and privileged access.[4] This element of experience will come into prominence in a couple of chapters. Hence the level of presentations can be formulated thus (Lonergan does not say much about utterances, nor will I):

Level of presentations

Imagination

Sense data

The level of intelligence is broached, as already seen, by the question for understanding. It is the question that moves the human knower out of the animal world of biological extroversion and sense experience to wonder about what has been presented. The question gives rise to a tension and a heuristic process, more a native cunning in common sense, but elaborated in specific methods in mathematics and science. This tension comes to an end with the desired insight; the insight, in turn, is expressed in the universal concept. The level of intelligence, then, can be formulated in three substages:

Level of intelligence

Concept

Insight

Question for information

---

[4]See above, p. 14–15, 41.

Once again the hypothetical play of insight is rudely broken through by a question for reflection. Is that so? Is it really true? The answer to that question is the judgment, which affirms, "Yes, it is so," or "No, it is not so," or some midjudgment of "perhaps," or the withholding of a judgment. But between the question for reflection and the issuance of the judgment intervenes a process that Lonergan calls reflection proper, whereby evidence for the proposed judgment is produced and weighed. Lonergan gives this a sustained treatment in the following chapter. The process can once more be summarized in three steps:

Level of reflection

Judgment

Reflection

Question for reflection

If the three levels are conflated, Lonergan's overall analysis of the human knowing process appears:

Level of reflection

Judgment

Reflection

Question for reflection

Level of intelligence

Concept

Insight

Question for information

Level of presentations

Imagination

Sense data

It may not be amiss to remind the reader that the point here is not to read Lonergan as though he were writing about a foreign country the reader has never visited. He is rather referring to processes every knower should have a certain familiarity with, even though they may never have been the subject of explicit or sustained attention. Hence the reader will enter into the spirit of Lonergan's inquiry only by asking such questions as, "Do I make judgments?" "Do I jump to conclusions?" "Do I always insist on having the evidence before I judge?"

Summary

Lonergan's analysis arrives at a certain fullness in the treatment of judgment in Chapter IX. Judgment is, in the first place, the final stage in the process of knowing; once a judgment is made, the process must start over again. But judgment is also the capstone of knowing, so Lonergan is prepared to reveal the total structure of human knowing.

Questions for Reflection

How does Lonergan's emphasis on judgment set him off from other modern philosophers?

Lonergan has been quietly assembling the overall structure of knowing. At what point did he introduce each element?

Chapter 8

How Does One Become a Person of Good Judgment?

READING: *Insight*, Chapter X, pp. 304–24 (279–99):
The General Form of Reflective Insight;
Concrete Judgments of Fact; Insights into Concrete
Situations; Concrete Analogies and Generalizations;
Common-Sense Judgments

As seen in the last chapter, the level of reflection unfolds in three stages: the question for reflection, the reflection itself, and the actual judgment. Of these, the question for reflection merely sets the stage by challenging the insight or concept: "Is it so?" On the other hand, the judgment is the affirmation that marks the end of the process, saying "Yes (it is so)" or No (it is not so)." Clearly, the key moment is the second. What happens between the question for reflection and the judgment? This is the crucial factor; in

Accordingly, the present section will be an effort to determine what precisely is meant by the sufficiency of the evidence for a prospective judgment. Presupposed is a question for reflection, "Is it so?" A judgment follows, "It is so." Between the two there is a marshaling and weighing of evidence. But what are the scales on which evidence is weighed? What weight must evidence have if one is to pronounce a *Yes* or a *No*? 304 (279) terms of knowing, one might say, "The buck stops here." Consequently, this chapter is extremely important to Lonergan's whole analysis of cognition.

The process has to do, first of all, with evidence. The question for reflection asks whether an insight is correct or not; the judgment will affirm or deny it. But this affirmation or denial will be arbitrary and unjustified unless the proper evidence is present.

Reflection, then, grasps the sufficiency of the evidence for the judgment. Like the grasp of pattern on the level of intelligence, this reflective grasp can also be called an insight. But the reflective insight should be carefully distinguished from the ordinary insight on the level of intelligence.

The Syllogistic Form of Judgment

But what is this reflective process like? How can one identify it in one's own cognitional process? Paradoxically, the clearest example, and the first one Lonergan gives, is a logical one. As mathematics and science have recognized methods to lead from the question for intelligence to the insight, so logic is a technique for providing explicit evidence for a judgment. The standard form is the syllogism:

All men are mortal.

Socrates is a man.

Therefore Socrates is mortal.

The conclusion, the last statement, is the judgment. What is the evidence for the judgment? It is supplied by the premises. The major premise is a general statement about humanity, known by induction. The minor premise identifies this individual with the species, man. The middle term, men, is particularly important in a syllogism. Unless "man" and "men" refer to the same nature, unless "man" is a subset of, or "falls under" "men," then the syllogism doesn't "work," it's invalid.

The "therefore" refers to a certain necessity; the conclusion is "implied" in the premises. In other words, if it is true that "All men are mortal," and if it is true that "Socrates is a man," then it is also necessarily true that Socrates is mortal.

Of course, this necessity is not absolute, but conditional. Socrates might not have existed; in fact, he did. It is also true that men are created mortal, but in another universe they might have been created immortal. (In fact, Socrates argues that man is immortal in his soul, though not in his body.)

Perhaps to underline this conditional necessity, Lonergan prefers the hypothetical form of the syllogism:

If X is material and alive, X is mortal.

But men are material and alive.

Therefore, men are mortal.[1]

This conditional necessity is not merely in the syllogism; if it is to be true, it must be reflected in some way in reality. The implicative force of the syllogism, then, echoes a prior conditional necessity in reality.

The Virtually Unconditioned

This is what Lonergan is referring to when he speaks of the "virtually unconditioned," which may sound like a strange term to refer to a judgment. But the virtually unconditioned is simply another name for a conditioned necessity. It is not an absolute necessity—only God is absolutely necessary. But, once a reality exists, it has a conditioned necessity; it might not have been; it might have been other than it is, but, in fact, it does exist, and exists in this particular way.

The syllogism is a clear way of exhibiting this conditioned necessity. It comprises three elements. The conditioned is the judgment to be made: "Therefore, men are mortal." The link between the conditioned and its conditions is the major premise: "If X is material and alive, X is mortal." The fulfillment of the conditions is given in the minor premise: "But men are material and alive."

---

[1]306 (281).

The conditioned, then, or the prospective judgment, has its conditions, because it is not absolutely necessary, but those conditions are in fact fulfilled, so the conditioned can legitimately be affirmed.

From this one instance emerges the general structure of providing evidence for a judgment: It will always be a virtually unconditioned, that is, a conditioned whose conditions are identified and fulfilled.

Though the syllogism brings out this structure very clearly, it remains highly artificial. Except when they want to be particularly precise and technical, people do not normally justify their judgments by drawing up an explicit syllogism. Indeed, a person makes many judgments in a day, and it would be exceedingly tedious to try to justify each one by verbalizing a syllogism.

Further, it can be shown that the syllogism cannot be the final form of reasoning. It results from the simple reflection that it takes two premises to ground one conclusion. Suppose one wants to explicitly justify the major premise of a syllogism. This will require two prior premises. And to ground the minor premise, another two premises will be required. So to ground two premises requires four prior premises, and grounding those would require eight premises, and those sixteen—and so on. Obviously, the number quickly mushrooms toward infinity, indicating that complete logical grounding is an impossible process.

The Practical Form of Judgment

Much more common than the logician's syllogism is what Lonergan calls the concrete judgment of fact. The example he gives on pages 306–7 (281) may be symbolized in this form:

[If the same thing shows two different characteristics at different times, then something has happened.]

[But this house shows two different characteristics at different times.]

Therefore, something happened.

As Lonergan observes, this is about as simple a concrete judgment of fact as one can get. In some ways, the structure here is continuous with that analyzed above. There is a conditioned: "Something happened." There is a link between conditioned and conditions: "If the same thing shows two different characteristics at different times, then something has happened." The fulfillment of the conditions is also given: "But this house shows two different characteristics at different times."

What is different in the concrete judgment of fact, however, is that, as indicated by the brackets, the two premises are not made explicit. The person does not come home and think, "Now let's see, what was that rule about something happening? Oh yes, that's it. Now, can I say that this condition is fulfilled? Yes, I have now a minor premise. So I can validly draw the conclusion, 'Something happened.'"

No, the judgment is made spontaneously and almost immediately. The major premise is simply a habitual and implicit judgment that is present in the mind, based on observation since childhood, and probably never explicitly formulated. Again, the conditions are fulfilled as soon as the person sees the house: It is obviously different from when the man left it.

But what was explicitly present as evidence in the two premises of the syllogism is therefore much more implicit in the mind and in sense experience. So the question returns more insistently: "How is the sufficiency of evidence grasped in a reflective insight?" "How does a person know that the evidence, presented only implicitly, is indeed strong enough to make the affirmation?"

The Accuracy of Insights

Ultimately, the level of judgment offers as its direct content only a *Yes* or a *No*." So Lonergan turns his attention back to the level of insight. How is one sure that the original insight is correct? Lonergan distinguishes between an invulnerable and a vulnerable insight. One is safe in making a judgment if one's insight is invulnerable. Such is Lonergan's first answer to the validity of judgment.

But that, of course, only pushes the question further back. How does a person know that his insight is invulnerable? An insight is invulnerable, Lonergan answers, when there are no further, pertinent questions. This makes sense in terms of Lonergan's analysis of cognitional process thus far. Questions give rise to insights, and a new insight would complement or challenge an older one. If there are no further questions, then one may assume no complementary or contradictory insights will arise, and so the original insight will be invulnerable.

Of course, the qualifying word *pertinent* must also be noted. There are always some further questions. But the criterion of the invulnerable insight is that there are no more pertinent questions that might lead to further, qualifying insights.

But the question only seems to be pushed further back. How does one know that there are no further, pertinent questions? The obvious first answer is, "If no further relevant questions occur; if a person can't think of any further, pertinent questions." But Lonergan is not satisfied with that more subjective criterion. He wants an objective criterion: There simply are no further, relevant questions.

> Note that it is not enough to say that the conditions are fulfilled when no further questions occur to me. The mere absence of further questions in my mind can have other causes. My intellectual curiosity may be stifled by other interests. My eagerness to satisfy other drives may refuse the further questions a chance to emerge. To pass judgment in that case is to be rash, to leap before one looks.[2]

On the other hand, Lonergan holds that it is too much to require the absolute impossibility of further questions. Good judgment, then, is a matter of balance. One must have more than a simple absence of questions, especially if that absence is grounded in a deliberate lack of curiosity. Yet human knowing cannot

---

[2]309 (284).

demand an absolute impossibility of further questions: It is almost impossible to prove such a negative.

Once again, however, the question seems to be pushed back a further step. How is a person to attain such a sense of balance? How does one know when it has been reached in a particular case? Lonergan proposes no one simple answer to this question, but a number of contributing elements. Indeed, there can be no simple, logical answer; one moves here more in the realm of practical wisdom or prudential judgment. "But how is one to strike this happy balance between rashness and indecision? How is one to know when it is reached? Were there some simple formula or recipe in answer to such questions, then men of good judgment could be produced at will and indefinitely."[3]

Four Elements of Good Judgment

The first element Lonergan points to is openness to truth. The drive to know has already been spoken of. It is that intellectual energy which gives rise to questions in the first place, which is expressed in the wonder of the scientist and the philosopher, which is the motive keeping people working day and sometimes night to find the treasure of knowledge. "The seed of knowledge has to grow into a rugged tree to hold its own against the desires and fears, conations and appetites, drives and interests, that inhabit the heart of man."[4] That pure desire to know must be given free rein, must be more than a passing quest in a person's mind. Truth must be sought, to put it another way, and truth-seeking must become habitual. Part of that giving free rein to the pure desire to know is to allow the further questions and further insights to arise, and to integrate them with what is already known.

The second element of Lonergan's answer is acquired expertise in a particular area. In the simple case of concrete judgment considered, that was hardly necessary. Anyone of moderate intelligence and no special training would be able to recognize that

---

[3]310 (285).
[4]Ibid.

"something happened" to the man's house. But many judgments are much more complicated and require a great deal of specialized training. Is this nuclear reactor about to overheat? One would not consult a shoe repairman for an answer. Is the timing belt in this automobile poorly adjusted? One would probably not ask a sugar cane–cutter. But there are judgments on which the shoe repairman and the farmer would be the experts. The rule, then, is that a person is able to make trustworthy judgments in those areas in which he has a full familiarity, a special training, a particular expertise.

Note that this division of labor has a presupposition: The universe of our experience can be broken down into areas of expertise and mastered piecemeal. So it is not necessary to know everything about cutting sugar cane before learning about automobiles, or to know all about shoe repairing before becoming a nuclear engineer. Still, that division of areas also provides a caution: Shoemaker, stick to your last!

The Self-Correcting Process of Knowing

How does one gain such expertise? The question is answered by Lonergan's third element, the self-correcting process of learning. No one is born with a particular expertise. Yet some people have clearly mastered a field. How does one get from one state to the other? By the self-correcting process of knowing. Sometimes that takes place by simple experience. Sometimes one accompanies a past master, watching, trying, picking up hints, profiting from corrections. At other times the process is formalized: an apprenticeship, a school, a residency. In any case, it follows a typical curve: From initial, bungling attempts it rises more and more quickly toward a point where the apprentice becomes the master, the pupil the teacher. No one, of course, knows everything, but the master usually knows what is up, what the alternatives are, which one to try first, where the relevant information may be found, whom to consult in a particularly perplexing case.

The process is called *self-correcting* because it is usually not a smooth, upward curve. Almost inevitably, one makes mistakes. But that does not mean learning is permanently stymied. Indeed, one often learns most from one's mistakes, integrating those lessons as well into the self-correcting process of knowing.

To summarize Lonergan's answer, then, to how one knows that no further, relevant questions exist, he says that a person is in a position to make that determination when he or she has been faithful to the pure desire to know, and is judging in a particular area in which he has attained mastery through the self-correcting process of learning.

At this point Lonergan returns to the question of temperament. Even with the three elements already mentioned, some persons still tend to judge too quickly, while others hesitate unreasonably. This brings Lonergan to the fourth and final element of his solution: There must be a personal wisdom by which one has come to know one's own personal temperament, and allows for its potential distortion of the cognitional process.

Further Aspects of Judgment

The rest of the material may be covered more expeditiously. Lonergan has a brief section on generalizations, which should be fairly straightforward. There is the legitimate principle that similars are similarly understood. But there are also two caveats. On the one hand, this presumes that the insight into the first situation is correct, which brings one back to the analysis just completed. On the other hand, there must be a true similarity between the two situations; any significant dissimilarity may invalidate the judgment.

Lonergan then goes on to speak of commonsense judgments and their relation to scientific ones. After making the important point that learning is a social as well as an individual project, he comes to the disputes between common sense and science. As seen already, common sense remains in a familiar world, whereas science moves, often fairly quickly, into a recondite world of specialized jargon, mathematical equations, and realities that cannot even be imagined. A statement in this scientific language can sometimes seem to run clearly contrary to common sense.

One famous example involves Galileo. His scientific studies convinced him that the earth revolved around the sun. But the

Common sense, then, has its own specialized field or domain. It has its own criteria on the relevance of further questions. It has its own basically constant vocabulary, its proper universe of discourse, and its own methodological precepts of keeping to the concrete, of speaking in human terms, of avoiding analogies and generalizations and deductions, of acknowledging that it does not know the abstract, the universal, the ultimate. Precisely because it is so confined, common sense cannot explicitly formulate its own nature, its own domain, its own logic and methodology. These it has to learn, if it would limit properly its pronouncements, but it has to learn them in its own shrewd fashion through instances and examples, fables and lessons, paradigms and proverbs, that will function in future judgments not as premises for deductions but as possibly relevant rules of procedure. Finally, because common sense has to be acquired, it is not possessed equally by all. It has its adept pupils who make mistakes, indeed, but also learn by them. Within their familiar field they are masters, and as well they know that they must master their own hearts, that the pull of desire, the push of fear, the deeper currents of passion are poor counselors, for they rob a man of that full, untroubled, unhurried view demanded by sure and balanced judgment. 322 (297)

church, basing itself on the commonsense language of the Bible, insisted it was the sun that rose and set. Thus a contradiction between common sense and scientific language became also a struggle between science and religion.

Lonergan addresses this conundrum by distinguishing ordinary description and explanation. Ordinary description is the commonsense relation of things that are already familiar to us. Explanation, on the other hand, is the scientific mode of discourse where things are related to each other. Conflict can be avoided, then, if every statement of common sense is preceded by the qualification, "From the point of view of ordinary description...," and every scientific statement by the qualification, "From the point of view of explanation...." Consequently:

> From the viewpoint of explanation, the planets move in approximately elliptical orbits with the sun at their focus.

> From the viewpoint of ordinary description, the earth is at rest and the sun rises and sets.[5]

Summary

As judgment is the final step in knowing, so the ultimate justification of knowing must be sought in the grounding of the judgment, which Lonergan treats in Chapter X. A judgment is grounded by grasping its sufficient evidence, which emerges most clearly in a syllogism; it is also present in the practical judgment, whose premises are usually implied.

Assessing a sufficiency of evidence brings one back to the accuracy of the prior insight. An insight is accurate if it is invulnerable; it is invulnerable if there are no further, pertinent questions. Establishing the lack of further, pertinent questions requires a general openness to truth; possibly training in a particular area, gained through the self-correcting process of knowing, and a familiarity with one's typical tendency to rashness or overcaution. As is clear, making good judgments is rarely a simple logical process.

Questions for Reflection

What does Lonergan mean by "sufficiency of evidence"? The "virtually unconditioned"?

How does Lonergan try to strike a happy balance between a mere subjective absence of questions and the demonstrated impossibility of further questions?

What elements are involved in becoming a person of good judgment?

---

[5]320 (295).

Chapter 9

Suiting the Action to the Word

READING: *Insight,* Chapter XI, pp. 343–62 (319–39):
Self-Affirmation of the Knower

Lonergan asks the reader to make a crucial judgment in Chapter XI. The relatively long commentary will be divided into two parts: Preliminaries to the Judgment, and The Judgment Itself.

I. Preliminaries to the Judgment

With Chapter XI, the reader has come to the heart of Lonergan's book. Indeed, in the introduction,[1] Lonergan states that, from a formal logical point of view, the first judgment is made in Chapter XI. The first part of the book, the analysis of cognitional process, has concluded; the second part, in which Lonergan proceeds to construct his philosophy on that basis, is beginning.

In the first part, the object of the insights was in various fields: mathematics, physics, common sense. But, as has been stressed, the central emphasis all along has been, not the content of the insights, but the act of insight itself; the fields chosen served more to provide examples because obviously an insight has to be an understanding of something. But now not only is the act of

---

[1] 17 (xxii).

insight to be considered, but its content will be insight (and the rest of the knowing process) itself.

At a number of points above it was mentioned that, besides the experience delivered by the five senses, there was also an experience of cognitional process itself, by which the knower has an individual and privileged access to his own knowing activities.[2] If there were a reader who did not have such an access to his own knowing, the whole first part of *Insight* would have made little if any sense; it would be like giving a disquisition on color to a blind man. But for most readers, it is hoped, the cognitional analysis of the first part has heightened this native awareness of what is going on *within one's head* when one is engaged in knowing.

Applying the Structure of Knowing to Itself

Again, in chapter 1 of this study it was noted that human knowing has the unique ability to "return upon" itself.[3] In Chapter XI Lonergan exploits this capacity. To put it another way, what Lonergan is doing is turning on itself the structure of knowing diagramed above in chapter 7.

To spell this out more concretely, the knower is aware of his or her sense experience. A person can vary that at will by the simple expedient of opening and closing his eyes or covering his ears. The knower also experiences the operation of his imagination; persons—some more than others—can, at will, picture this or that in full color. A knower can also experience the tension that is questioning. It can be a very unsettling, restless desire that will drive a person for hours and hours to find out what is the case; should he finally decide to give up, because it is simply taking too long, that too will probably not be accomplished without a pang of regret. But then comes the sweet satisfaction of having an insight! The more frustrating and prolonged the searching, the more joyous the "eureka!" It is hoped that the reader will have

---

[2]See above, pp. 14–15, 41, 64.
[3]See above, p. 15.

had that satisfaction relatively frequently in reading these pages because, like all teaching, they are intended to occasion insights. The knower will also have had the experience of realizing that an insight into a particular case also has a universal relevance. No doubt the reader will also have experienced that roadblock in the knowing process of the reflective question, the imperious "Is that so?" "Are you sure?" "What is the evidence?" The judicious reader will also recognize the process by which the evidence for a prospective judgment is weighed. Finally, the knower will no doubt remember the experience of making many judgments in his or her life, most trivial, some of them weighty, many correct and perhaps not a few of them wrong.

Moreover, it is also possible to understand all these activities. In fact, anyone who read the preceding paragraph attentively and intelligently will have understood what sense experience is, what imagination is, what the question for intelligence is, what insight itself is, what the process of conception is, the question for reflection, the weighing of the evidence, and the actual judgment.

Insight into Insight

The alert reader may remember that, in his preface, Lonergan promised an "insight into insight." Perhaps the intervening investigation will have clarified somewhat that initially obscure reference.

Further, the knower will have grasped that an insight has potentially a universal significance, far beyond any particular

> The affirmation to be made is a judgment of fact. It is not that I exist necessarily, but merely that in fact I do. It is not that I am of necessity a knower, but merely that in fact I am. It is not that an individual performing the listed acts really does know, but merely that I perform them and that by "knowing" I mean no more than such performance. 343 (319)

situation or set of elements that has been understood. To give a more specific example, the reader will grasp that what has been said above applies to any act of sense experience, any act of imagination, any act of questioning, any act of insight, any act of conception, any act of reflective questioning, any act of weighing the evidence, and any act of judgment.

Still further, reflective questioning may be applied to the structure of knowing. Is there such a thing as sense experience? Does the knower really have a faculty called imagination? Do I question? Is it true that sometimes I have insights? Have I ever asked a reflective question? Do I in fact weigh the evidence for a judgment? Do I actually make judgments?

Finally, judgment can be applied to the process. The knower can judge that he enjoys sense experience. He can affirm the existence of imagination in his knowing. He can assert that indeed he questions. He can claim to have had insights. He can say that he knows what it is to have a universal concept. He can insist that he does ask reflective questions and judiciously weighs the evidence. Last, he can make the judgment that he makes judgments.

It is the complex of judgments made in the last paragraph that is the "first judgment," already referred to, that Lonergan proposes in Chapter XI. Or, to put it in other terms, the judgment in question is the affirmation of the structure of cognitional process.

The Proposed Judgment in Syllogistic Form

Lonergan sets this up in the more formal way that should already be familiar from the past two chapters. First, there is a conditioned: "I am a knower." Next, there is a link between the conditions and the conditioned: "I am a knower, if I am a concrete and intelligible unity-identity-whole, characterized by acts of perceiving, imagining, inquiring, understanding, formulating, reflecting, grasping the unconditioned, and judging." Finally, there is a fulfillment of the conditions: "I do experience acts of perceiving, imagining, inquiring, understanding, formulating, reflecting, grasping the unconditioned, and judging."

This may be represented syllogistically as follows:

I am a knower, if I am a concrete and intelligible unity-identity-whole, characterized by acts of perceiving, imagining, inquiring, understanding, formulating, reflecting, grasping the unconditioned and judging.

[But I do experience acts of perceiving, imagining, inquiring, understanding, formulating, reflecting, grasping the unconditioned, and judging.]

Therefore, I am a knower.

Lonergan does not make much of the first premise. "Similarly, the link offers no difficulty; the link itself is a statement of meaning; and the conditions which it lists have become familiar in the course of this investigation."[4] In other words, Lonergan is simply offering here a definition of knowing. His syllogism is to the effect: If knowing is constituted by these activities, and if I perform these activities, then I am necessarily a knower.

The reader will have noted that the minor premise has been placed in brackets. This does not mean it exists in quite the implicit way that the principle of change exists in the mind of the man returning home. Lonergan has in fact formulated the premise on the pages of his book. But the *evidence* for the minor premise is not a formulation or set of formulations; it is simply the *experience* of those activities, as presented above. So the evidence for the reflective question of whether I enjoy sense experience is simply the awareness of doing so; the evidence for the reflective question of whether I have insights is simply the experience of having insights; the evidence for whether I have concepts is the experience of conception, and so on.

---

[4] 344 (319).

Consciousness

On pages 344–52 (320–28) Lonergan gives some observations preliminary to the formal judgment. The first concerns consciousness. As already noted, Lonergan has a pervasive polemic against the simplistic notion that "knowing is looking." If knowing were looking, then consciousness would be "looking at looking." But if knowing is sense experience, imagination, question, insight, concept, reflective question, weighing the evi-

> We have been engaged in determining what precisely is meant by consciousness. We have contended that it is not some inward look but a quality of cognitional acts, a quality that differs on the various levels of cognitional process, a quality that concretely is the identity immanent in the diversity and the multiplicity of the process. However, one cannot insist too strongly that such an account of consciousness is not itself consciousness. The account supposes consciousness as its data for inquiry, for insight, for formulation, for reflection, for grasp of the unconditioned, for judgment. But giving the account is the formulating and the judging, while the account itself is what is formulated and affirmed. Consciousness as given is neither formulated nor affirmed. Consciousness is given independently of its being formulated or affirmed. To formulate it does not make one more conscious, for the effect of formulation is to add to one's concepts. To affirm it does not make one more conscious, for the effect of affirmation is to add to one's judgments. Finally, as consciousness is not increased by affirming it, so it is not diminished by denying it, for the effect of denying it is to add to the list of one's judgments and not to subtract from the grounds on which judgments may be based.   350 (326)

dence, and judgment, then consciousness is sense experience, imagination, question, insight, concept, reflective question, weighing the evidence, and judgment of sense experience, imagination, question, insight, concept, reflective question, weighing the evidence, and judgment.

Lonergan also points out that there are levels of consciousness; each level of knowing activity has its proper kind of awareness.[5] So on the level of sense and imagination, the knower is aware in the mode of biological extroversion, which man has in common with the other animals; Lonergan calls it "empirical consciousness." On the level of intelligence, the knower is aware in the mode of intelligent consciousness, and on the level of reflection, he is aware in the mode of rational consciousness.

Further, Lonergan points out, these consciousnesses exhibit a unity. I do not sense one thing, turn around and understand something completely different, and then make an affirmation about some third, totally unrelated reality. Rather I sense something, I try to get a grasp of it, and I ask, "Is *that* true?" and make a judgment on that precise subject.

Behind this unity is an "I." It is I who have the sense experience, the same I who try to understand and sometimes succeed, and the same I who make judgments. Nor is the unity something merely concluded to. As a unity already given in consciousness, it too might be placed in brackets. [I am the unity who senses, understands and judges.] Once again, when one pushes the bases of human knowing, one arrives at a point when not everything can be fully and logically formulated. "What do I mean by 'I'? The answer is difficult to formulate, but strangely, in some obscure fashion, I know very well what it means without formulation, and by that obscure yet familiar awareness, I find fault with various formulations of what is meant by 'I.'"[6]

II. The Judgment Itself

This brings Lonergan to the affirmation itself. "I am a knower." As is true of the whole book, of course, the point is not that Lonergan should make the affirmation, it is that the reader

---

[5]346 (322).
[6]352 (328).

should. But, after all this elaborate buildup, the answer is almost so obvious as to be an anticlimax.

> Does consciousness supply the fulfillment for the other conditions? Do I see, or am I blind? Do I hear, or am I deaf? Do I try to understand or is the distinction between intelligence and stupidity no more applicable to me than to a stone? Have I any experience of insight, or is the story of Archimedes as strange to me as the account of Plotinus' vision of the One? Do I conceive, think, consider, suppose, define, formulate, or is my talking like the talking of a parrot? I reflect, for I ask whether I am a knower. Do I grasp the unconditioned, if not in other instances, then in this one? If I grasped the unconditioned, would I not be under the rational compulsion of affirming that I am a knower and so, either affirm it, or else find some loop-hole, some weakness, some incoherence, in this account of the genesis of self-affirmation? As each has to ask these questions of himself, so too he has to answer them for himself. But the fact of the asking and the possibility of the answering are themselves the sufficient reason for the affirmative answer.[7]

A Privileged Judgment

After having made the judgment of the affirmation of cognitional process, Lonergan goes on to show how this is a privileged, a self-authenticating, and in some ways an unavoidable judgment. Perhaps a way to grasp this will be to return to a detail of the analysis above, in which the activities of knowing were systematically applied to the activities of knowing. Passing over the question of whether there is a sense experience of sense experience, or an imagination of imagination, certainly one can raise a question about questioning, can have an insight into insight, a concept of the concept, a reflective question about whether reflective questions exist, a weighing of the evidence for the weighing of evidence in human knowing, and a judgment about judgment. All these are particular aspects of the fact that human knowing turns upon

---

[7]352–53 (328).

itself. But, while these all make perfect sense, their opposites are simply incoherent. Could there be a question that seriously ques-

> Am I a knower? The answer *Yes* is coherent, for if I am a knower, I can know that fact. But the answer *No* is incoherent, for if I am not a knower, how could the question be raised and answered by me? No less, the hedging answer "I do not know" is incoherent. For if I know that I do not know, then I am a knower, and if I do not know that I do not know, then I should not answer. 353 (329)

tions whether questions are totally nonexistent? Could there be an insight into the total absence of insight? A concept of the nonexistence of conception in the universe? A reflective question whether there might be no reflective questioning? A weighing of the evidence for a total lack of weighing the evidence? A judgment that there is no judgment?

As is obvious, the very act would be an annulling, a contradiction, of the content of that act. Question whether questioning exists, and at least one question exists. That is an example of conditional necessity. Questioning might never have existed. But once I ask a question, it is obvious that at least one example of questioning exists. Similarly, if I have an insight into the absence of insight, I have produced at least one existing insight, which destroys the absence. If I have a concept of a total lack of conception, then at least one concept exists, which shows that lack is not so total after all. If I ask a reflective question whether reflective questioning is a myth, I have produced at least one reflective question and so undermined the myth. If I weigh the evidence for a lack of weighing the evidence, then I have adduced at least one example of weighing the evidence, and so have begun to supply that supposed lack. Finally, if I judge that there is no such thing as judgment, I have contradicted myself because I have, willy-nilly, exhibited the existence of at least one judgment. Again, one supports the judgment of cognitional process by examining the alternatives. Will anyone seriously claim to neither see nor hear nor smell nor taste nor feel? Helen Keller was both blind and deaf, but someone was ultimately able to help her to understand the use of words and concepts through the sense of touch. Would anyone insist that he was totally without imagination, unable to imagine anything in any way at all? Would anyone claim to be so inert and stolid and incurious that he had never in his life asked a question? Would anyone want to claim he was so stupid as never to have understood a single thing? Would anyone seriously say that he had never noted that there were repetitive kinds of things in the universe, that the same word could apply to each of them, and that an insight into one was potentially relevant to all the rest? Could anyone really say he had never wondered whether something was true, or asked for the evidence for a proposition? Could anyone say he was so irresponsible that he had never weighed the evidence before making a statement? Could anyone with the least bit of sobriety or self-awareness claim to have never made a judgment?

Lonergan points out that the knowing process is part of natural law.[8] As kittens have to crawl, so human beings have to know. I cannot simply decide one day that I am tired of being a knower, that from now on I will content myself with being merely an animal or a vegetable. I would literally have to do physical violence to myself to attain that aim. And then, with the last flickers of disappearing human consciousness, I would probably wonder whether this was such a smart thing to do.

A Science of Knowing

In the next section[9] Lonergan broaches the notion of a science of cognitional process. The path that physical science has trod from commonsense experience—description, or the relation of things to us—to scientific formulation—explanation, or the relation of things to each other—has already been noted. This

---

[8]353–57 (329–32).
[9]357–59 (332–35).

suggests to Lonergan that a similar path may lead from a common-sense grasp to a scientific formulation of inner experience. But there would be this difference: The basic categories of physical science are always subject to revision, but those of inner science, once they are precisely formulated, will be "locked in place," because of the self-authenticating nature of the judgment of self-affirmation. If the fundamental terms of knowing are sense, imagination, question, understanding, concept, reflective question, weighing the evidence and judging, then it would be incoherent to use those activities to ground some differing account of cognitional process.

Next[10] Lonergan shows the impossibility of revising the affirmed structure of knowing by analyzing the very notion of "revision." For why do people revise an account? If an account is perfectly and fully satisfactory, there is no need to revise it; to do so, in fact, would be silly and would risk ending in error. No, an account is revised only if there is something wrong with it. Typically, one wishing to revise an account points to data that have been overlooked. Or one may concede that the data are complete, but that they have been misunderstood. On the basis of further data, or a new understanding of the original data, one makes a new and different judgment. But this shows that the very anatomy of revision implies data (experience), understanding (insight) and judgment. So how is one to use the structure of experience, understanding and judgment to revise the structure of experience, understanding and judgment?

Still again,[11] Lonergan shows how this same inevitability results from the very notion of a judgment of fact. A judgment of fact affirms a *Yes* or a *No* about something. But the "something" is not supplied by the level of judgment which, properly speaking, offers only the *Yes* or *No*. So the judgment presumes a prior level of understanding. But, if the judgment is not to be arbitrary, there has to be some evidence for it, some fulfilling of conditions, some data on which it is based. But data are given on the level of experience.

---

[10]359–60 (335–36).
[11]360–62 (336–39).

So the very possibility of making a judgment of fact, then, requires a prior level of intelligence and of presentations, once more validating as inevitable the structure of experience, understanding and judgment.

The Ultimate Ground of Knowing

Finally, one further implication of the self-authenticating nature of the structure of knowing should be mentioned. If the structure of knowing cannot coherently be used to deny the structure of knowing, it is also true that the structure of knowing cannot be used to give some further, or especially, some logically unassailable grounding to the structure of knowing. The reason is obvious: The grounding can only be attempted through the process of knowing, but then the grounding can be no more sure than the process itself.

To put that another way (perhaps it is not so obvious!), it will be remembered that the validation of knowing was based on conditional necessity. *If* there is a concept, it cannot be the concept of the total lack of concepts. But this is not absolute proof that there must be such a thing as a concept; it is merely an argument that an existing concept is incompatible with a total lack of concepts. Again, *if* an insight exists, then that insight cannot coherently be the grasp of the impossibility of insights. But this does not prove that there must be an insight in the first place. Once more, *if* there is a judgment, it would be silly for its content to be the absence of judgment in the universe. A universal negative is annulled by any one positive example, and the judger would, in this case, inevitably be supplying his own counterexample. But this does not mean that judgment necessarily exists.

The point has already been made in a number of ways: Logical demonstration cannot be the ultimate form of knowing, and human intelligence cannot ground itself with apodictic necessity. Hence, Lonergan concludes:

> Self-affirmation has been considered as a concrete judgment of fact. The contradiction of self-negation has been indicated. Behind that contradiction there have been discerned natural

inevitabilities and spontaneities that constitute the possibility of knowing, not by demonstrating that one can know, but pragmatically by engaging one in the process. Nor in the last resort can one reach a deeper foundation than that pragmatic engagement. Even to seek it involves a vicious circle; for if one seeks such a foundation, one employs one's cognitional process; and the foundation to be reached will be no more secure or solid than the inquiry utilized to reach it. As I might not be, as I might be other than I am, so my knowing might not be and it might be other than it is. The ultimate basis of our knowing is not necessity but contingent fact, and the fact is established, not prior to our engagement in knowing, but simultaneously with it. The sceptic, then, is not involved in a conflict with absolute necessity. He might not be; he might not be a knower. Contradiction arises when he utilizes cognitional process to deny it.[12]

Summary

From general considerations on knowing in the first half of the book, Lonergan in Chapter XI turns to a concrete judgment by a concrete person, inviting the reader to affirm: "I am a knower." If the reader is not a knower, of course, such a judgment would be incorrect. Still, one couldn't be a reader without knowing something! Not only, then, can the reader make the judgment: The judgment is self-authenticating in that trying to deny it is contradictory. The contradiction, however, is not one between two statements; it is a contradiction of one's simple existence as a knower. Thus Lonergan proposes a science of knowing, whose basic principles will be unrevisable, but he also points out that there is no deeper proof of knowing than one's simple existence as a knower.

---

[12]356–57 (332).

Questions for Reflection

What precisely does Lonergan mean in this chapter by "being a knower"?

What is the relation of Lonergan's "I am a knower" to Descartes' "I think, therefore I am"?

Why is physical science revisable, but Lonergan's proposed science of knowing not so?

Chapter 10

If I'm a Knower, What Do I Know?

READING: *Insight*, Chapter XII, pp. 372–88 (348–64):
A Definition; An Unrestricted, Spontaneous,
All-Pervasive but Puzzling Notion

Having established the structure of knowing in the previous chapter, Lonergan begins with Chapter XII to consider the known, assuming that the reader has agreed with the analysis of cognitional structure, and made an affirmation of that structure based on the evidence of his or her own mind. But Lonergan has a peculiar approach to what we know when we sense, inquire, understand, conceive, ask the reflective question, weigh the evidence and judge. He does not start at the obvious place of considering zebras and cacti, telephone poles, running shoes and rock cliffs. Rather he remains with the structure of knowing that he has so carefully analyzed.

Being Defined in Terms of Knowing

Getting this unusual approach will be difficult, especially for someone familiar with a more traditional entrée to metaphysics. Perhaps an analogy will help. A locksmith has a key and a lock to study. He is really interested in the lock. But, for the time being, he sets the lock aside and studies the key, which will necessarily say something about the inner structure of the lock. Applying the analogy, knowing is the key, and the known is the lock. Lonergan has analyzed the structure of knowing and wants now to study the known. But he does not immediately pick up the lock; rather, he sets it momentarily aside to see what can be known of the lock by the structure of knowing.

For Aristotle, metaphysics is the basic science. How did he come to his insights about being in the most universal and abstract sense of the word? Broadly oversimplifying, perhaps the genesis of the thought was something like this. The Platonic dialogues already show an interest in classification. How does one grasp things by kinds? Start, for example, with spiders. A person encounters one spider, then another and another. After a while, kinds of spiders are recognized: a black widow or a brown recluse and so forth. Then one realizes that spiders also have something in common: They all have eight legs, for example. But spiders fit into larger classifications: that of all insects, for example. But insects fit into the classification of animals, and animals into that of living things. Suppose this movement upward through the classifications continues. Where will it end? Obviously, when everything in the universe is taken together at once. At that point, what characteristic do they all share in common? The answer is that they exist. Whatever it is, it has this unique property, that it *is*. Things that are merely conceived or imagined do not have this property. So the most basic consideration is *being*, which is the basic notion of Aristotle's metaphysics.

Being Defined from Knowing

But Lonergan does not follow this particular route. He does not abstract to being by starting from things. Rather he comes to being by considering the process of knowing.

The pure desire to know has already become familiar. It is the intellectual energy that serves the whole structure of knowing, goading on the knower from sense experience to asking questions, to having insights to conceiving their universal import, to wondering whether indeed they are valid to weighing the evidence and

The desire to know means the dynamic orientation manifested in questions for intelligence and for reflection. It is not the verbalizing of questions. It is not the conceptual formulation of questions. It is not any insight or thought. It is not any reflective grasp or judgment. It is the prior and enveloping drive that carries cognitional process from sense and imagination to understanding, from understanding to judgment, from judgment to the complete context of correct judgments that is named knowledge. The desire to know, then, is simply the inquiring and critical spirit of man. By moving him to seek understanding, it prevents him from being content with the mere flow of outer and inner experience. By demanding adequate understanding, it involves man in the self-correcting process of learning in which further questions yield complementary insights. By moving man to reflect, to seek the unconditioned, to grant unqualified assent only to the unconditioned, it prevents him from being content with hearsay and legend, with unverified hypotheses and untested theories. Finally, by raising still further questions for intelligence and reflection, it excludes complacent inertia; for if the questions go unanswered, man cannot be complacent, and if answers are sought, man is not inert.   372–73 (348)

making judgments. It is also the thrust that goes beyond any particular judgment to ask still further questions. As hard as it works to attain a particular insight, it never seems to be satisfied, but is already restlessly looking beyond this insight, like a man at a cocktail party, who has just met one person, but is already looking over that person's shoulder toward someone else.

"Being, then, is the objective of the pure desire to know."[1] So Lonergan defines being, not by abstracting from particular things, but by beginning with the universal thrust of the pure desire to know. The result is that being is not concretely specified as yet. To put it in Lonergan's more technical terminology, this is a definition of the second order.[2] Being is the object of the pure desire to know.

---

[1] 372 (348).
[2] 374 (350).

But the pure desire to know is prior to any particular act of knowing, so the known of the definition is completely open. What precisely the known is remains to be determined by particular activities of knowing. When this is done, it will inevitably be some component of being, because the activities of knowing are placed into motion only through the pure desire to know, and being is the object of that pure desire to know; so whatever is discovered through that process will belong to being.

> What is this objective? Is it limited or unlimited? Is it one or many? Is it material or ideal? Is it phenomenal or real? Is it an immanent content or a transcendent object? Is it a realm of experience, or of thought, or of essences, or of existents? Answers to these and to any other questions have but a single source. They cannot be had without the functioning of the pure desire.[3]

Being Is Universal

Lonergan goes on to note that being embraces all that is known, as well as all that is to be known.[4] Being includes all that is known because whatever is known is known by the operation of the knowing structure. But the knowing structure is driven by the pure desire to know, and being is the object of the pure desire to know. But being also includes whatever will be known. For something will be known by the same process and structure of knowing. But that will be put into motion only by the pure desire to know, and being is defined as the object of the pure desire to know.

There is a further implication. The pure desire to know works only through the structure of knowing. But that operation never comes to any closure except through a judgment, which marks the end of one episode of the knowing process. So being can also be defined in terms of judgments. Being is the object of all the judgments I have made; it is also the object of all

---

[3] 373–74 (349).
[4] 374 (350).

the judgments I will make or could ever conceivably make. More fully, being is the object of all true judgments.

Lonergan does not make the point here, but the same argument could be made for insight. The pure desire to know operates through the structure of knowing, which inevitably includes a moment of insight. So being is also the object of all accurate insights.

Being as All-Embracing

Lonergan next goes on to show that being is all inclusive. He does this largely by posing objections. They can all be summed up in the final objection: "Suppose X is beyond being." But all that is necessary is to ask, "What is X?" For the pure desire to know also operates through questions for understanding. Therefore, the object of any question for understanding is being.

It is true, of course, that there may be misformed or incoherent questions. But that too will only be discovered by the operation of the pure desire to know. Being has been defined, not as the object of all formulated questions, but as the object of the pure desire to know, which is prior to all formulated questions. Still, one may say that being is the object of all well-formulated questions.

To systematize slightly more than Lonergan does, being can be defined in four different ways, all equivalent, of which the primary definition is the first. So being is:

—the object of the pure desire to know;

—the object of all true judgments;

—the object of all accurate insights; and

—the object of all well-formulated questions.

In each case, however, it will be noted, the known has been determined through the process of knowing.

Being as a Spontaneous Notion

Next Lonergan goes on to speak of being as a spontaneous notion. The convention has already been used to place in brackets what is spontaneously present and operative in the mind even before it is formulated, even if it is never formulated; the reader will recall the principle of change in chapter 8 [If the same thing shows two different characteristics at different times, then something has happened], or the notion of consciousness in chapter 9 [But I do experience acts of perceiving, imagining, inquiring, understanding, formulating, reflecting, grasping the unconditioned, and judging].

But the pure desire to know is similar. Lonergan has obviously formulated it in his book. But even before it was formulated, it was operative in Lonergan's mind, even when he was a five-year-old boy. Again, the reader may now have formulated for himself this pure desire to know, but before he did so it was already operative in his mind, and, if it had not been operative, the reader would never have arrived at the point of formulating it. So this prior and spontaneous operation may be designated [the pure desire to know]. It is not the desire as formulated, at least in the first instance, of which being is the object; it is the object of the desire as spontaneously operative. This means that being is not merely what philosophers talk about or seek; every knower is headed toward being, although he may be able to define neither "knowing" nor "being," much less the "pure desire to know." Being itself, then, as the object of the [pure desire to know] will have a certain spontaneity about it; it is intended whether or not a knower has formulated it; it is, in short, also [being]. That is what Lonergan means by a spontaneous notion of being.

The reader should further note that Lonergan gives to "notion" an unusual and idiosyncratic meaning. Normally "notion" is a vague thought about something. But Lonergan is using it as an orientation, a heading toward. But what is it that heads for [being]? It is the [pure desire to know]. So the "notion of being," in Lonergan's specialized sense, turns out to be [the pure desire to know] itself. As spontaneous, that could also be designated as a [notion].

After having pointed out that the notion of being, in his specialized sense of the pure desire to know as heading toward its objective, underpins and penetrates all cognitional contents,

Perhaps it is this internal conflict that has led some to the conclusion that a false judgment is meaningless. But such a conclusion seems astoundingly false. Were the false judgment meaningless, there would be nothing to be false. The false judgment is false precisely because it means a state of affairs that is the opposite of the state one intends to affirm, namely, the state that truly is. 382 (358)

indeed constituting them as cognitional,[5] he goes on to treat of meaning.[6] Again, Lonergan defines meaning in terms of cognitional structure.

After answering a number of puzzles about being,[7] he spends the rest of the chapter examining various theories of being. Besides the spontaneous notion of being, there are also formulated accounts. Lonergan has given his, and now he compares and contrasts it with that of other philosophers.[8]

Summary

Lonergan turns from knowing to the known in Chapter XII, but he remains true to his unique approach through the subject. The known will be the object of knowing, so being is the object of the pure desire to know. Being is all-embracing because whatever exists can become the object of the pure desire to know. The pure desire to know is also a spontaneous notion because it exists and operates before anyone tries to formulate it.

Lonergan has formulated his account of being; that account may then be compared with that of other philosophers.

------

[5]380–81 (356–57).
[6]381–83 (357–59).
[7]383–88 (359–64)
[8]388–98 (364–74).

Questions for Reflection

How is Lonergan's own definition of being continuous with his previous analysis of knowing?

In what four equivalent ways may being be defined?

Chapter 11

True Objectivity Is Authentic Subjectivity

READING: *Insight,* Chapter XIII, pp. 399–409 (375–84):
The Principal Notion of Objectivity; Absolute,
Normative and Experiential Objectivity

Chapter XIII continues Lonergan's exploration of the known by raising the question of objectivity. For if the known is merely a subjective persuasion, and not a knowing of objective truth, it would not be worth much. Once again, however, Lonergan attempts to define objectivity in terms of the structure of knowing.

Initially, that may seem to be a very unpromising approach. If we are seeking objectivity, why would we look for it in the knowing subject? We distinguish between objectivity and subjectivity. Surely subjectivity would be sought in the subject, but why would objectivity?

What Is Objectivity?

But what, after all, is objectivity? Suppose I have before me three objects: a small statue, a candle, a cowbell. Are they objective? Is the objectivity in the objects? Does the simple presence of the objects guarantee objectivity? That does not seem right either. Somewhat like the old conundrum of whether a tree falling in the forest generates a sound if no one is there to hear it, objectivity, paradoxically, requires a subject to be objective.

A young child lives partly in a fantasy world and partly in the real world. At times an imaginary playmate may seem even more vivid than a real one. But maturing as a knower requires learning to discriminate sharply between fantasy and reality. Fantasy is subjective; reality is objective. But note that this growing ability is not in the objects surrounding the child, nor even in the objects of his imagination. The growing sense of objectivity, then, is in the maturing child.

What constitutes this sense of objectivity? It is, first of all, the child's ability to distinguish himself and the products of his fantasy from the real world around him. Second, what is gained is something of a reconciliation, even a resignation, to reality itself. One realizes that one cannot shape the world of reality in the same way a fantasy can be shaped, at will, and that a tantrum is not going to change a reality, however distasteful it may be to the child. (Of course, this maturity is often not complete; a Walter Mitty type can continue to live in a fantasy world, even as an adult; more destructively, a person may be in denial of a reality that would seem to be staring him in the face.)

Objectivity and Judgment

Objectivity, then, consists in distinguishing oneself from other things. How is this done? Lonergan points to the intellectual activity of judgment, which has a certain objectivity about it. By judgment, the knower affirms that something simply is, that something is true, that it is a fact, whatever might be the preferences or the predilections of the knower himself.

The judgment, as already seen, requires evidence. The knower cannot simply say, "I affirm this, because I wish it to be so." No, he has to find and recognize the evidence before pronouncing, "This is so"; otherwise his affirmation is arbitrary.

So far the knower has been asked to make one judgment: "I am a knower." To reach the basic state of objectivity, then, only two further judgments are required: "Something else is"; "I am not that something." This is the basic minimum for being able to affirm that something is, irrespective of my own imagination or desires. Of course, over a lifetime one has not only affirmed oneself, but many other realities. And so objectivity is constituted by the context of all those judgments that affirm the self, affirm other realities and affirm the difference between them.

A Spontaneously Operative Notion

So there is in the knower a spontaneously operative notion of objectivity, and it is not necessarily opposed to the one Lonergan has formulated. "In brief, there is objectivity if there are distinct beings, some of which both know themselves and know others as others."[1]

What is it about the judgment that gives it this basic objectivity, that allows objectivity to arise in a suitable context of judgments? It is that the judgment affirms the virtually unconditioned. It is a cognitional act that has corresponding to it in reality a conditioned necessity. I am a knower. I didn't have to exist, and I didn't have to be a knower. But, in fact, I am a knower. However conditioned, this is now a necessity. Similarly, to use the example Lonergan does, once Caesar crosses the Rubicon, it will forevermore be true that he has done so; he may apologize for it, but he may not undo the act. Anyone thereafter who affirms it is telling the truth, and anyone who denies it is telling a lie. It is this necessity, grasped and affirmed in judgment, which is the very basis of objectivity.

But the pure desire to know, it will be remembered, is the motive power of the knowing structure, and so it too is related to objectivity. For the pure desire to know not only drives toward judgment, but it does so in a normative way. It demands attention to the original data; it calls for rigorous questioning; it seeks accurate and apposite insights; it urges the question for reflection; it presides over the weighing of the evidence, and ensures a valid judgment. Mistaken judgments exist, but they usually arise when

---

[1] 401 (377).

the knower is unfaithful to that pure desire, allows other desires and wishes and biases to interfere with it, so that data are overlooked or inattentively scrutinized, or questions are arbitrarily brushed aside, or insights embraced too quickly because they are gratifying, or the question "Is it so?" is not resolutely pressed, or the evidence is perfunctorily weighed, or contrary evidence simply excluded, so that the judgment does not represent the proper unfolding of the pure desire to know. Both objectivity and subjectivity are grounded in the knower: objectivity in fidelity to the pure desire to know, subjectivity in listening to the siren call of other wayward desires and biased wishes.

Lonergan's Treatment of Objectivity

In the chapter Lonergan presents these ideas more formally. He begins with the principal notion of objectivity, that which

Sixth, the principal notion of objectivity solves the problem of transcendence. How does the knower get beyond himself to a known? The question is, we suggest, misleading. It supposes the knower to know himself and asks how he can know anything else. Our answer involves two elements. On the one hand, we contend that, while the knower may experience himself or think about himself without judging, still he cannot know himself until he makes the correct affirmation, "I am," and then he knows himself as being and as object. On the other hand, we contend that other judgments are equally possible and reasonable, so that through experience, inquiry and reflection there arises knowledge of other objects both as beings and as being other than the knower. Hence we place transcendence, not in going beyond a known knower, but in heading for being, within which there are positive differences and, among such differences, the difference between object and subject. Inasmuch as such judgments occur, there are in fact objectivity and transcendence. Whether or not such judgments are correct is a distinct question to be resolved along the lines reached in the analysis of judgment. 401–2 (377) results from a context of a number of judgments. This is objectivity in the full sense of the word. But this is based on the absolute objectivity of the single judgment, which affirms something absolute, grasping and formulating the conditional necessity of the virtually unconditioned. Next he moves to normative objectivity, which is grounded in the pure desire to know.

When he comes to experiential objectivity, Lonergan is returning to the theme of the two kinds of knowing, of which he has said little in the recent chapters. As there are two kinds of knowing, the spiritual and the sensual, so there are two kinds of objectivity: that constituted by a pattern of judgments, and that constituted by biological extroversion. Is something true because I touch it? Or because I affirm it? Ideally, the two work together: The fact that I can touch it may be a key part of the evidence for affirming it. But two caveats should be mentioned: One is that there may be realities that I cannot touch, but which I may nevertheless affirm. Modern science, as already seen, exhibits some instances of this. The other is that, in human knowing, the ultimate criterion is the affirmation based on evidence; the sense datum enters only in a supporting role.

Lonergan makes some interesting points about experiential objectivity, the object of which he refers to as the "given." There is a certain passivity to sense experience. I do not cause it; it rather happens to me. In this there is a certain residual objectivity; my sensing is only in a limited way under my control. Studying the place of the given in the structure of knowing, it is clear that it is prior to questions. For that reason, it is also unquestionable. This does not mean that questions cannot be asked *about* it. In this way, it is the occasion for questions. But what Lonergan means is that the questions must assume it; they cannot undermine it because the given is given prior to any questions. Plato, it may be remembered, did question the deliverance of the senses. He said that the senses gave only what was shifting, temporary, undependable; truth was rather to be found in the intellectual world of the forms. Here Lonergan exhibits his concrete, Aristotelian bent: All knowing begins ultimately in the senses; as given prior to questions, the given is therefore unquestionable.

Moreover, the given is undifferentiated because differentiation is accomplished by selection and discrimination, and that requires insight. But the given is prior to insight. This is not to say the given cannot be understood, but merely that the given *as given* is prior to my understanding.

Summary

Lonergan tackles the question of objectivity in Chapter XIII. Paradoxically, he seeks it in the subject rather than in objects because objectivity does not inhere in objects; it is rather an achievement of the knower.

Questions for Reflection

What, after all, is objectivity?
How does Lonergan approach the question of objectivity?
What four aspects of objectivity does he distinguish?

Chapter 12

Can Knowing Reveal the Metaphysical Structure of Being?

READING: *Insight,* Chapter XIV, pp. 410–26 (385–401):
The Underlying Problem; A Definition of Metaphysics;
Method in Metaphysics

Chapter XIV of Lonergan's *Insight* serves to pull together many of the themes that have been presented piecemeal and in isolation previously in the book. In many ways, this chapter may be seen as the culmination of Lonergan's argument; the rest of the book merely works out the implications of what is established here. Indeed, Lonergan himself says much the same: "In the present chapter, then, an attempt will be made to define metaphysics, to state its method, and to clarify the method by contrasting it with other methods. In subsequent chapters the method will be articulated by an outline of metaphysics, a sketch of ethics, and a presentation of transcendent knowledge."[1]

Three Themes Recapitulated

Already in the introduction to *Insight* the theme of the duality of human knowing was sounded.[2] It was reinforced in chapter 2[3]

---

[1] 414–15 (389–90).
[2] See above, p.18.
[3] See above, p. 27.

and echoed in the distinction between "thing" and "body," substance and appearance, in Lonergan's Chapter VIII,[4] only to
appear once more in chapter 11.[5] Here it reappears as the basic
antithesis Lonergan formulates at the beginning of the chapter.
There is the contrast of the notions of objectivity, already noticed:
one based on the full context of human knowing, anchored in a
patterned set of judgments, and the other based on animal or
sense extroversion. Again, the being defined by the pure desire to
know is set against the "already out there now real" discovered by
sense. Once more, the clear affirmation of the structure of knowing is contrasted to the confusion of intellectual and sense knowing. Lonergan introduces here the word *polymorphism,* which is a
new term, but not a new thought. It merely implies that in the
human being two kinds of knowing exist, and that, until a careful
investigation is made, the two tend easily to be confused.

The same basic contrast of two kinds of knowing is at play
when Lonergan comes to distinguish position and counterposition.[6] A position is a philosophical stance that is based on, or
coherent with, the full structure of human knowing, while a counterposition will be based on some partial grasp of the knowing
process, typically one that equates knowing with "looking."

Priority of the Intellectual Pattern

A second theme resumed in this chapter is the priority for
Lonergan of the intellectual pattern of experience, already noted.[7]
Here he says:

> The intellectual pattern of experience is supposed and
> expressed by our account of self-affirmation, of being, and of
> objectivity. But no man is born in that pattern; no one
> reaches it easily; no one remains in it permanently; and when

---

[4]See above, pp. 53–59.
[5]See above, p. 104.
[6]413 (387–88).
[7]See above, pp. 51, 52, 58.

some other pattern is dominant, then the self of our self-affirmation seems quite different from one's actual self, the universe of being seems as unreal as Plato's noetic heaven, and objectivity spontaneously becomes a matter of meeting persons and dealing with things that are "really out there."[8]

A third theme, stressed from the beginning of this commentary, is that Lonergan's philosophy is a personal achievement. The reader is not merely to take Lonergan's word for the process of cognition, but to verify it in his or her own consciousness. In treating of the method of metaphysics, Lonergan insistently resounds this theme:

Further, the subject that is envisaged is not some general or transcendental or absolute subject; from the viewpoint of the writer it is any particular subject that can experience, can inquire intelligently, can reflect critically; but from the viewpoint of the reader the particular subject is the subject that he or she is.[9]

Bluntly, the starting point of metaphysics is people as they are.[10]

The process, then, to explicit metaphysics is primarily a process to self-knowledge.[11]

But the result can exist only in a self-affirming subject, and the process can be produced only by the subject in which the result is to exist. It follows that the directives of the method must be issued by the self-affirming subject to himself.[12]

To recapitulate, the goal of the method is the emergence of explicit metaphysics in the minds of particular men and women. It begins from them as they are, no matter what that may be.[13]

---

[8]410–11 (385).
[9]421 (396).
[10]422 (397).
[11]Ibid.
[12]423 (398).
[13]426 (401).

An Approach to Metaphysics

The subject of this chapter is the generation of philosophy, or more specifically, metaphysics. Philosophy or metaphysics is what is known by a philosopher. To that extent, Lonergan is turning from the knower to the known. Not surprisingly, however, he keeps to his habit of first investigating it, not from all the philosophies that are known, but from the process of knowing itself. It may seem hopelessly ambitious to try, not merely to produce one's own philosophy, but also to account for all the other strands and varieties in human history. That is, it seems hopelessly ambitious until one remembers that every philosophy is produced by a human mind. Further, that mind has a structure, as revealed in Chapter XI. And

> In the light of the dialectic, then, the historical series of philosophies would be regarded as a sequence of contributions to a single but complex goal. Significant discoveries, because they are not the prerogative of completely successful philosophers, are expressed either as positions or as counterpositions. But positions invite development, and so the sequence of discoveries expressed as positions should form a unified, cumulative structure that can be enriched by adding the discoveries initially expressed as counterpositions. On the other hand, since counterpositions invite reversal, a free unfolding of human thought should tend to separate the discovery from its author's bias in the measure that its presuppositions are examined and its implications tested. 414 (389)

so every philosophy will either be in accord with that structure—a position—or it will constitute a living contradiction to that structure—a counterposition. That is Lonergan's basic insight.

Is Metaphysics Feasible?

Philosophy has often been despaired of. It seems like an endless cacophony of discordant voices, which never appears to make any progress. Unlike the physical sciences which, despite occasional errors and false pathways, clearly have made immense advances since their beginnings in the seventeenth century, philosophy appears ever again to rehearse the same basic arguments; in every generation the same positions are presented once more and controverted just as quickly.

Lonergan disagrees with this assessment, which overlooks the difficulty of the project. The method of science remains constant, even as its discoveries pile up. But the scope of philosophy is so broad—it takes as its subject literally everything—that the method and the results are on the same scale. It is as if a workman were forced to create his tool at the same time he was pursuing his project.

Further, Lonergan argues, this dismal assessment overlooks the fact that the discordant voices may be presenting incomplete views on a larger subject. The five blind men returning from an investigation of the elephant did not report something completely untrue; each had a piece of the truth, only mistaking it for the whole. Their seemingly discordant reports could still be integrated into an accurate whole. In a somewhat similar way, the philosophers—many of whom were brilliant thinkers—might each have grasped something of the knowing process, mistaking it for the while, but that glimpse of the truth can still be integrated into a complete account of knowing.

Lonergan does admit that his approach makes a key presumption: "However, the dialectic itself has a notable presupposition, for it supposes that cognitional theory exercises a fundamental influence in metaphysics, in ethics, and in theological pronouncements."[14] This will be recognized as the assumption underlying Lonergan's approach in all the recent chapters, trying to discern something of the known by examining the process of knowing.

A Definition of Metaphysics

Lonergan next goes on to develop a definition of metaphysics. In the process, once again, Lonergan seems almost to

---

[14] 414 (389).

change the meaning of the word. Metaphysics is usually thought of as a set of propositions within the covers of a book. Without excluding that meaning, Lonergan is envisioning, in the first instance, something prior to that, something present and spontaneously operative in the mind. To use the convention already adopted, Lonergan is speaking of a [metaphysics]. "It underlies all other departments, for its principles are neither terms nor propositions, neither concepts nor judgments, but the detached and disinterested drive of the pure desire to know and its unfolding in the empirical, intellectual and rational consciousness of the self-affirming subject."[15] More specifically, Lonergan denotes this sense of metaphysics as "latent metaphysics." "For latent metaphysics is the dynamic unity of empirical, intellectual, and rational consciousness as underlying, penetrating, transforming, and unifying the other departments of knowledge."[16] In other words, just as the notion of being is spontaneously present and operative in

> Second, the major premise is the isomorphism that obtains between the structure of knowing and the structure of the known. If the knowing consists of a related set of acts and the known is the related set of contents of these acts, then the pattern of the relations between the acts is similar in form to the pattern of the relations between the contents of the acts. This premise is analytic. 424 (399)

everyone's mind, whether he or she is a philosopher, so is this latent metaphysics present in everyone's mind.

The notion of the heuristic has already been introduced in chapter 3. It is the characteristic of inquiring intelligence by which the mind grasps, not the answer itself, but some anticipation of its shape or location. Here Lonergan appeals to the same notion, but in a generalized way. For the object of metaphysics is

---

[15]415 (390).
[16]417 (392).

being, everything. So the structure of knowing that seeks it is universal; it is the "integral, heuristic structure."[17]

From Latent to Explicit Metaphysics

Lonergan's metaphysical method, finally, is a move from latent to explicit metaphysics, or from [metaphysics] to metaphysics. It begins with the knower as subject, before any precision is gained about the knowing process. The process is spontaneously operative, but it is not grasped and formulated. Naturally, this is no simple process, so it will in all likelihood go through an intermediate, problematic stage before arriving at a full and satisfactory account.

An explicit metaphysics that manages to grasp and formulate the [metaphysics] spontaneously operative in the human mind will, naturally, be in accord with that spontaneously operative structure of knowing. To put it in the terms used earlier in the chapter, it will be a position. Any explicit metaphysics that is in disaccord with the spontaneously operative structure of knowing will, of course, be a counterposition. Consequently, Lonergan holds that his method, which moves from latent to explicit metaphysics, is the only philosophical method that is not arbitrary. "For there is only one method that is not arbitrary, and it grounds its explicit anticipations on the anticipations that, though latent, are present and operative in consciousness."[18]

As Lonergan spent the remainder of Chapter XII in comparing and contrasting his account of being with that of other philosophers, so in the rest of Chapter XIV he compares the method presented here with that followed by other philosophers.

Summary

Making explicit a dichotomy that has been gradually emerging, Lonergan contrasts the objectivity grounded in judgment with

---

[17]416 (391).
[18]427 (402).

animal extroversion, the being that is the object of the pure desire to know with the "already out there now real" encountered by sense, and the clear formulation of the structure of knowing with the confused polymorphism of an undifferentiated consciousness. In each case, the first represents the position, the second a counterposition.

Lonergan proposes a metaphysics based on the position; it will be grounded in the very structure of the mind as operative. Metaphysics will heuristically anticipate the structure of the known that is already revealed in the structure of knowing. Having formulated his own account of metaphysics, Lonergan turns to comparing it with that of other philosophers.

Questions for Reflection

In what basic contrasts does Lonergan summarize his treatment of knowing?

How is metaphysics a personal achievement?

What marks Lonergan's unique approach to metaphysics?

Chapter 13

So What Is the Structure of the Known?

READING: *Insight,* Chapter XV, pp. 456–63,
507–11 (431–37, 483–87):
Potency, Form and Act; Central and
Conjugate Forms; Summary

"As the preceding chapter outlined a programme, so the present chapter turns to its execution."[1] This sentence beginning Chapter XV reinforces the idea that Lonergan's basic argument is essentially complete by Chapter XIV.

What Lonergan attempts in the early part of Chapter XV is to work out the basic structure of the physical universe. By this

> Metaphysics has been conceived as the integral heuristic structure of proportionate being. It envisages an indefinitely remote future date when the whole domain of proportionate being will be understood. It asks what can be known here and now of that future explanation. It answers that, though full explanation may never be reached, at least the structure of that explanatory knowledge can be known at once. 456 (431)

---

[1]456 (431).

time the reader will not be surprised to learn that he does so, not by studying the universe, but by examining the process of knowing.

Isomorphism of Knowing and Known

In chapter 10, above, the image of the key and the lock was introduced.[2] Knowing is the key to which the universe is the lock. By examining the key, it is possible to fix certain main features of the lock.

In Chapter XIV,[3] and in the summary of Chapter XV, Lonergan speaks of the isomorphism of knowing and known. *Isomorphism* comes from two Greek words, *isos,* meaning same (as in isosceles triangle) and *morphe,* which means form. Isomorphism, then, refers to things that are the same or similar in form. If the structure of the universe is similar to, or the same as, the structure of the knowing process, then one may deduce certain fundamental features of the universe from the characteristics of cognitional process.

The Triadic Structure

The structure of knowing is basically triadic: experience, insight and judgment. So the basic structure of the universe may also be expected to be basically triadic. There must be something corresponding to experience; Lonergan calls it potency. It is potential because, as it is experienced through sense extroversion, it is what can be understood, but is not yet understood. It is only in actually understanding that something corresponding to insight appears, which Lonergan calls form. Again, that name fits because what an insight grasps is a pattern in previously disparate and unorganized data. Finally, as insight calls out, through the reflective question, for judgment, so form evokes something corresponding to judgment. Lonergan calls it "act." Once more, a certain appropriateness obtains, because a form is merely a possibility, sharing

---

[2]See above, pp. 92–93.
[3]424–25 (399–400).

the hypothetical nature of insight. "Act" is what allows the positive answer to the question, "Is it so?" Act is what takes form from the shadowy world of possibilities, to introduce it into the hard world of fact.

Lonergan goes on to argue that potency, form and act form a unity. This is also deduced from the fact that experience, insight and judgment form a unity. It is not one thing we experience, and then a totally other we understand, and then something else again on which we pronounce judgment. Rather, the insight depends upon its prior and corresponding experience, and this judgment presumes its prior and corresponding insight. Otherwise there would be no materials to understand, no insight on which to pronounce judgment. But, if the structure of knowing is a unity, then, from the isomorphism of knowing and known, the structure of the known as potency, form and act must also be a unity.

A Traditional Metaphysics

Those familiar with the Aristotelian-Thomistic tradition will recognize in Lonergan's categories of potency and form the Thomistic distinction of matter and form, and in Lonergan's form and act the Thomistic distinction of essence and existence. While basically accepting that substantial identification, Lonergan is also at pains to point out differences. These may, for present purposes, be left aside as a scholarly quibble, but what the reader may take away is that, if there are differences from Aristotle, it is because Lonergan so clearly differentiates sense and intellectual knowing and puts such a premium on the intellectual pattern of experience.

Lonergan, as seen above in chapter 6, makes a key distinction between substance and accidents, between the unity-identity-whole in data he calls the "thing," and the sense appearances, the object of sense extroversion, which he calls the "body." This division reenters here as the distinction of a twofold kind of potency, form and act. For if two different kinds of insight grasp the qualities of things as related, and the thing itself that is related, then there will be two different kinds of form. The more traditional terms will be substantial and accidental forms; Lonergan prefers to speak of central and conjugate forms. But if potency, form and act are a unity, then substantial form will imply a central potency and a central act. Central act is traditionally known as existence, *esse* in Thomas's Latin. Similarly, accidental or conjugate forms must have a corresponding potency and act. This did not receive as much attention in Thomas's analysis. Lonergan identifies conjugate act as "occurrence," whereas conjugate potency he assigns to the experiential aspect of spatiotemporal relations.

> The difference between our central form and Aristotle's substantial form is merely nominal. For the Aristotelian substantial form is what is known by grasping an intelligible unity, an *unum per se*. However, since the meaning of the English word *substance* has been influenced profoundly by Locke, since the Cartesian confusion of *body* and thing led to an identification of substance and extension and then to the riposte that substance is underneath extension, I have thought it advisable, at least temporarily, to cut myself off from this verbal tangle. 462 (436)

Terminological questions arise here once more. In chapter 6 the position was taken that the traditional "substance" was preferable to Lonergan's "thing." In this case "central form" seems a helpful substitute for "substantial form." Lonergan gives his criticism of "accidental": "The name, accidental, is misleading for it suggests the merely incidental."[4] But one may wonder whether "conjugate," though founded in Lonergan's thought, adds anything to clarity.

In summary, whatever the quibbles about terminology, it is clear that the basic elements of metaphysics are six: substantial or central potency, form and act, and accidental or conjugate potency, form and act.

---

[4] 462 (437).

Retrospect

At the end of the chapter Lonergan offers another of his help-ful summaries. First, he restates his definition of metaphysics. Then he presents the movement from a latent to an explicit metaphysics in a military metaphor of breakthrough, envelopment and confine-ment. The breakthrough is achieved in Lonergan's Chapter XI on self-affirmation, which again underlines that this chapter is at the heart of Lonergan's argument. The envelopment is identified with Chapter XII, which grasps the known of being, defined at a second remove as whatever is the object of the pure desire to know. Finally, the confinement takes place in Chapter XIV, which sets up most formally the contrast of the two kinds of knowing, and the two notions of reality and objectivity that flow from them.

Lonergan reviews the six metaphysical elements on page 510 (486), and then goes on to specify what exactly is meant by the isomorphism of knowing and known. It is not that one may make a deduction from a whole set of ideas on the mind, which are then to be found in reality in a detailed way, as Leibniz tried to do. The structure of the knowing process does not reveal the details of the known, but only its most general features.

> The correct locus of the parallel is to be found in the dynamic structure of our knowing. Inquiry and understanding presup-pose and complement experience; reflection and judgment presuppose and complement understanding. But what holds for the activities, also holds for their contents. What is known inasmuch as one is understanding, presupposes and comple-ments what is known by experiencing; and what is known inasmuch as one is affirming, presupposes and complements what is known by understanding.[5]

Summary

At the beginning of *Insight* Lonergan promised an empiri-cally grounded metaphysics, and here he fulfills that promise. He

---

[5] 511 (486).

presents the six basic metaphysical realities, which closely parallel the Aristotelian and especially the Thomistic elements. Yet Lonergan educes them from the three stages of cognitional process, and the distinction between the insight into relations and the insight into the unity-identity-whole that is substance.

Questions for Reflection

What does Lonergan mean by "the isomorphism of knowing and known"?

If the structure of knowing is unrevisable, and the structure of reality is educed from the structure of knowing, does that mean Lonergan's metaphysics is also unrevisable?

Conclusion:
Retrospect and Prospect

In casting a glance back at this survey of Lonergan's *Insight,* the first thing that may be stressed is its incompleteness. Whole swaths of the book, at beginning and end, were neglected. Even in the pages covered, more difficult notions were ignored or insufficiently explained. Nuance was often sacrificed in the interests of clarity. To contend fully with Lonergan's thought would require that all these difficulties be faced, and the popularizer always faces the danger of so simplifying the master's thought as to render it questionable or even ludicrous.

Looking Back

Nevertheless, it is hoped that this survey view of *Insight* will reveal the basic structure of Lonergan's argument, one that obviously begins with the knowing process. As Lonergan says, "However, the dialectic itself has a notable presupposition, for it presupposes that cognitional theory exercises a fundamental influence on metaphysics, in ethics, and in theological pronouncements."[1] This starting point is one many more traditional Thomists would question. From the analysis of cognitional process Lonergan moves toward a philosophical performance, the self-affirmation of the knower, in which he invites the reader to participate, while

---

[1] 414 (389).

showing the inevitabilities of the nature of knowing that precede, accompany and defend that performance.

Once the knowing process is grasped and affirmed, Lonergan then exploits it to discern heuristically the basic structures of the known, all by appealing to the structure of knowing itself. So, in turn, he treats of being, of objectivity, of metaphysics and of the basic elements of metaphysics. In his preface, Lonergan claims that his method will yield an empirically based philosophy.[2] The meaning of that claim may now be clearer. For Lonergan begins with an empirical investigation—not the experience of the five senses or the outer world, but the experience of cognitional process, an "inner experience." So he is making claims that the reader is invited to verify for himself. His original appeal, then, is not to the memory of some Platonic heaven, nor to some blinding intuition of reality, nor to some uniquely persuasive set of ideas, but to prosaic facts of cognitional process that any knower can verify for himself.

Next, through the isomorphism of knowing and known, he deduces the basic structures of the to-be-known. So his metaphysical elements are ultimately reducible to the results of an empirical investigation.

Lonergan arrives at a metaphysical analysis similar to that of Aristotle and Thomas. But what they achieved by strokes of metaphysical genius, he corroborates through an empirical method.

> Seventhly, however, there is much to be gained by employing the method. Aristotelian and Thomist thought has tended to be, down the centuries, a somewhat lonely island in an ocean of controversy. Because of the polymorphism of human consciousness, there are latent in science and common sense not only metaphysics but also the negation of metaphysics; and only the methodical reorientation of science and common sense puts an end, at least in principle, to this permanent source of confusion. Further, without the method it is impossible to assign with exactitude the objectives, the presuppositions,

---

[2] 5 (xi).

and the procedures of metaphysics, and this lack of exacti-
tude may result in setting one's aim too low or too high, to
resting one's case on alien or insecure foundations, in pro-
ceeding to one's goal through unnecessary detours.[3]

Further Questions

Such a procedure raises an obvious and pressing question,
which can neither be passed over, nor can it be fully treated: "In
this process of trying to get at reality through the knowing
process, does Lonergan attain reality, or only his own mind?" The
similar, but closer-to-home question is, "Does the reader, in trying
to follow Lonergan's example, attain reality, or only his or her
own mind?" To put it another way, the presumption of the last
few chapters has been the isomorphism of knowing and known.
But how is the reader sure that the known corresponds in structure to the knowing process? More simply, how do we know that
the key fits the lock?

Lonergan himself seems to raise the question at a couple of
points in the book.

> An account has been given of a principal notion of objectivity
> and of its three partial aspects, the experiential, the norma-
> tive, and the absolute. However, there also exists subjectivity,
> and the reader may be inclined to find in the present section a
> full confirmation of a suspicion that he has for some time
> entertained, namely, that we have failed to place our finger on
> what is objective, that we are confusing with the objective
> either in part or in while what really is subjective.[4]

> Secondly, it may be asked whether the metaphysical elements
> constitute an extrinsic or an intrinsic structure of proportion-
> ate being. Are they merely the structure in which proportionate
> being is known? Or are they the structure immanent in the
> reality of proportionate being?[5]

---

[3] 425–26 (400–1).
[4] 407–8 (383).

Readers of Lonergan have sometimes been convinced that, in fact, he is an idealist who never does escape the confines of his own mind. The first article I wrote on Lonergan was published in the October 1972 issue of the *Thomist.* In a later, critical letter, Reverend G. H. Duggan, S.M., wrote, "From a host of passages in *Insight* it is clear that Lonergan, abandoning the realist epistemology of St. Thomas, starts, in Cartesian fashion, from the act of cognition and then strives, at great length but unsuccessfully, to pass from our knowing of being to being as it is in itself."[6] Finally to answer this question would require a much more penetrating assessment of Lonergan's *Insight* than was attempted here. Nevertheless, the reader may be left with a challenging question: "If the key does not fit the lock, then how would we know anything at all?"

---

[5] 522–23 (499).
[6] *Homiletic and Pastoral Review,* March 1974, p. 4.

Index

Symbolic, 3
Synthesis, 2, 3
System, 24, 30, 34
Systematic, 35, 48

Theological, 3, 7, 110, 120
Theoretical, 17, 49, 51
Theory, 61, 110, 120
Thomas Aquinas, 1–3, 15, 20, 27, 117, 121, 123
Thomist, 5, 121
Thomist, the, 123
Thomistic, 1, 2, 4, 116, 119
Thomists, 120
Transcendence, 11, 12, 103
Transcendent, 11, 12, 95, 106
True, 19, 32, 60, 61, 65, 68, 69, 75, 81, 84, 87, 89, 96, 98, 100–102, 104
Truth, 11, 48, 60, 73, 77, 100, 102, 104, 110

Unconditioned, 69, 70, 81–83, 85, 94, 97, 102, 104
Understanding, 5, 7, 10, 13, 14, 16–18, 21, 27, 31, 35, 37, 46, 48, 64, 78, 81, 82, 88, 89, 94, 96, 97, 105, 115, 118
Universal, 20, 42, 48–51, 56, 64, 76, 80, 81, 89, 93–95, 112
Universe, 40, 43, 49, 69, 74, 76, 86, 87, 89, 93, 108, 114, 115

Verified, 43, 58, 61
Viewpoint, 8, 20–22, 28–30, 33, 40, 52, 55, 77, 108
Vision, 15, 20, 27, 85

Wisdom, 42, 49, 73, 75